THE SCHOLASTIC
ART & WRITING AWARDS
PRESENTS

THE
BEST
TEEN
WRITING
OF
2014

Edited by
HANNAH JONES
2004 Scholastic Awards
Gold Medal Portfolio Recipient

**Scholastic
Art & Writing
Awards**

For information or permission, contact:
Alliance for Young Artists & Writers
557 Broadway
New York, NY 10012
www.artandwriting.org

Editor: Hannah Jones
Senior Manager, Programs: Scott Larner
Managing Editor: Lisa Feder-Feitel
Art Director: Meg Callery
Copy Editor: Ingrid Accardi
Production Assistant: Sazia Afrin
Cover art: *Speechless*, Drawing by Jordan Smith,
Grade 12, Age 17, Johns Creek, GA. 2014 Gold Medal

Anthology printing, August 2014
ISBN13: 978-0-545-81896-4
ISBN10: 0-545-81896-6

DEDICATION

The Best Teen Writing of 2014 is dedicated to Kay WalkingStick, whose work and career exemplifies the commitment to creative self-expression and originality that the Scholastic Art & Writing Awards seek to encourage and foster in the nation's young artists and writers.

Kay earned a Scholastic Award in 1948 and was honored this year with an Alumni Achievement Award during the National Ceremony at Carnegie Hall.

Kay has provided invaluable support to the Awards program through the years by serving as a National Art Juror, curating the Art.Write.Now.Tour 2014, and teaming with the Awards staff to promote the Awards to American Indian students as part of the Awards 2014 summer initiative, Start.Write.Now.

The Scholastic Awards thank Kay for providing an example to young artists and writers everywhere, and for giving her time and energy to the program to help recognize and showcase their tremendous achievements.

Kay WalkingStick is an artist and a professor emerita of Cornell University, and she has an honorary Doctorate of Humane Letters from Arcadia University. WalkingStick's work is included in many collections, both public and private, including the Metropolitan Museum of Art, and regularly shows at the June Kelly Gallery in SoHo. WalkingStick is currently preparing for a 2015 retrospective at the Smithsonian's National Museum of the American Indian in Washington, D.C.

WalkingStick received her Scholastic Art & Writing Award when she was 13 years old. She also served as an Awards juror in 2010 and 2013. WalkingStick graduated from Beaver College and received a Master of Fine Arts degree in painting from the Pratt Institute.

TABLE OF CONTENTS

III Dedication
VII About *The Best Teen Writing of 2014*
VIII About the Scholastic Art & Writing Awards
X The Best Teen Writing of 2014 Jurors
XII Editor's Introduction

Portfolio Gold

2 *Morral*, Shannon Daniels
4 *Conjoined*, Nathan Cummings
8 *We Don't Like You*, Jonathan Gelernter
14 *Sight Without Vision, Vision Without Sight*, Emma Hastings
18 *Home on the Range*, Jack Rayson
23 *The Balancing Act*, Haley Lee
26 *What I Know About River Fallwell*, Jackson Trice
31 *Oranges*, Hanel Baveja

Personal Essay/Memoir

34 *Nine Letter's War*, Emma Henson
37 *Lessons My Mother Taught Me*, Caroline Tsai
41 *Inside Phnom Penh*, Francesca Paris
47 *Unconfined*, Jade Young
53 *The Streets of Jerusalem*, Molly Breitbart
57 *Contagion*, Kain Kim
63 *The Great Grandfather of My Myths*, Emily Green
70 *The Feminist in Me*, Tuhfa Begum
76 *Mimi's Museum*, Nicholas Elder
79 *The Last Summer Leaf*, Spencer Grayson
83 *Memoir of Imagination*, Kelley Schlise

Humor

87 *Long-Awaited Aid Finally Reaches Flood-Ravaged Philippines*, Christopher Zheng
90 *The Tech-over*, Justin Wisnicki

Science Fiction/Fantasy

93 *In Memoriam*, Sarah Mughal
103 *Hungry House*, Gregory Nam
110 *The Ghost Singer*, Mairead Kilgallon

Persuasive Writing

115 *The Search for Intelligence Beyond the Fine-tuned Universe*, Jae Woo Jang

Flash Fiction

126 *The Thing About Apples*, Lily Gordon
129 *A Series of Crowded Places*, Ashley Israel
131 *Escape*, Justin Gainsley

Journalism

135 *Fracking Into the Future*, Ryan Chung
140 *I'm a He, Not a Question Mark: The Trans Community Reflects on Issues of Identity, Sex, and Gender*, Jackson Brook

Dramatic Script

151 *Of Misanthropy*, Philip Anastassiou

Poetry

159 *The Goldsmith*, Ayla Jeddy
160 *Insomnia*, Stephanie Guo
161 *Hurricane Kaoru*, Latroy Robinson
163 *Ordinary Travel*, Michael Shorris
165 *Racism in America*, Darrell Herbert
167 *The Walrus*, Robert Elliott Wyatt
168 *Rita Hayworth, Actress, 1947*, Emily Mack
170 *A Lesson in Accepting Departure*, Oriana Tang
172 *Oil*, Camila Sanmiguel
174 *Dolbear's Law*, Noa Gur-Arie
175 *Em*, Sophia Diggs-Galligan
177 *How Black Curls Were Invented*, Julia Tompkins
179 *This Is a Poem for Airing Dirty Laundry*, Michal Leibowitz

181 *Lost in Death Valley*, Ryan Jimenez Jenkins
184 *Cheeseburgers*, Alexander Zhang
186 *God's Fury (a haibun)*, Viviana Prado-Nuñez
187 *Watching Little Boys Become Monsters (or Maybe They Always Were)*, Ava Goga
189 *Cartography*, Alana Spendley
191 *Winter*, C. Sophia George
192 *They Sold Them Down the River for a Song*, George Counts
196 *Flowers in April*, Anna Sudderth
198 *The Two O's of Eyes*, Warren Kennedy-Nolle
200 *New Year, After You Go*, Emeline Atwood
202 *Saba, Grandfather*, Elizabeth Heym
203 *The Heliades Search for Phaethon*, Madeleine LeCesne
205 *Will*, Sarah Gamard
207 *Zeniths and Nadir*, Ashley Huang
210 *Miami as a Household*, Dalia Ahmed
211 *Picking Favorites*, Aileen Ma
214 *Journal*, Hadassah Amani
215 *From Penelope, to Odysseus Lost at Sea*, Zoe Cheng
217 *A Lesson on Astronomy*, Kyna Smith

Short Story
218 *Bad Dumpling*, Jackie Yang
226 *The Survivor*, Austin Wei
235 *Finally Getting It*, Rona Wang
243 *City Man*, Clay Space
251 *Tomorrowland Today*, Elizabeth Engel
255 *How to Become Yourself*, Holly Chen
262 *The Harvard Hopeful's Handbook*, Carolyn Kelly
269 *Maanvaasani*, Cara Maines

277 About the Authors
288 A Teacher's Guide
292 Regional Affiliates
303 Acknowledgments

ABOUT THE BEST TEEN WRITING OF 2014

The pieces featured in *The Best Teen Writing of 2014* were selected from work that earned National Medals in the 2014 Scholastic Art & Writing Awards. The Awards, a national program presented by the Alliance for Young Artists & Writers, identifies and showcases teenagers with exceptional artistic and literary talent. Founded in 1923, the program celebrates creative students and extends opportunities for recognition, exhibition, publication, and scholarships.

This year, 579 students earned National Scholastic Medals in writing categories. The works selected for this publication represent the diversity of the National Medalists, including age and grade, gender, genre, geography, and subject matter. They also present a spectrum of the insight and creative intellect that inform many Award-winning pieces.

A complete listing of National Medalists and online galleries of winning works of art and writing can be found on our website at **www.artandwriting.org**. Visit our site to see how to enter the 2015 Scholastic Art & Writing Awards, a list of our scholarship partners, and ways you can partner with the Alliance to support young artists and writers in your community.

Some of the writing selections have been excerpted. Go to **www.artandwriting.org/galleries** to read all of the work as it was submitted.

ABOUT THE SCHOLASTIC ART & WRITING AWARDS

Started in 1923 by Scholastic founder Maurice R. Robinson, the Awards are the nation's highest honor and largest source of scholarships for creative teenagers. All students in grades 7 through 12 are encouraged to apply. In partnership with more than 100 local organizations, the 2014 Scholastic Awards received 255,000 submissions across 28 art and writing categories.

Notable Scholastic Awards alumni include Andy Warhol, Kay WalkingStick, Richard Avedon, Truman Capote, John Updike, Sylvia Plath, and many more.

RECOGNITION The Alliance and our partners provided regional and national recognition to more than 68,000 teens in 2014.

The top 17,000 regional winners competed in the national competition—2,000 earned national medals and were celebrated at the National Ceremony at Carnegie Hall. A replay of the ceremony webcast can be viewed at **www.artandwriting.org/carnegiewebcast2014**.

EXHIBITION One thousand works were displayed at the Art.Write.Now.2014 National Exhibition at Parsons The New School for Design and Pratt Institute's Pratt Manhattan Gallery in New York City.

Art.Write.Now.2014, a traveling exhibition featuring a selection of National Award–winning work, will make stops at the Rhode Island School of Design in Providence, Rhode Island, the Salt Lake City Public Library in Salt Lake City, Utah, and the Catskills Art Society in Livingston Manor, New York. The U.S. Department of Education and the President's Committee on the Arts and the Humanities will also host National Award–winning work at a yearlong exhibition in Washington, D.C.

PUBLICATION This anthology, *The Best Teen Writing of 2014*, features a collection of our students' most exemplary writing works. The Alliance also features work by National Medalists in the National Catalog and on our website, **www.artandwriting.org/galleries**. Publications are distributed free of charge to schools, students, teachers, museums, libraries, and arts and community organizations. Copies of *The Best Teen Writing of 2014* are also available for purchase on Amazon.com.

SCHOLARSHIPS The Alliance distributes nearly a quarter of a million dollars in direct scholarships annually to National Award–winning high school seniors. Students also leverage their success in the Awards for funds from a network of sixty partnering universities, colleges, and art schools, which collectively earmark more than $8 million in financial aid.

NATIONAL STUDENT POETS PROGRAM In 2011, the President's Committee on the Arts and the Humanities and the Institute for Museum and Library Services partnered with the Alliance to create the National Student Poets Program (NSPP), the country's highest honor for youth poets presenting original work. Annually, five outstanding high school poets whose work demonstrates exceptional creativity, dedication to craft, and promise are selected for a year of service as national poetry ambassadors.

National Student Poets are chosen from National Medalists in the Scholastic Art & Writing Awards. Student Poets receive college scholarships and opportunities to present their work at writing and poetry events nationwide.

Visit **www.artandwriting.org/nspp** to learn more.

THE BEST TEEN WRITING OF 2014 JURORS

American Voices
Tanya Baker
Nell Beram
Annabeth Bondor-Stone
Daniel Ehrenhaft
Angie Frazier
Carole Geithner
David Krasnow
Jaclyn Moriarty
Carson Moss

Best in Grade
Kwame Alexander
Moira Bailey
Sharon Flake
Lisa Lucas
Kay Parks Haas
Lisa Schulman

Creativity and Citizenship
Naif Al-Mutuwa
Margi Preus
Duncan Tonatiuh

Dramatic Script
Carolyn Boriss-Krimsky
Blair Brown
Nora Quinn

Flash Fiction
Shelley Coriell
Hannah Jones
Vicky Shecter

Gedenk Award for Tolerance
Ramin Ganesharm
Elly Gross
Jennifer Lemberg

Humor
Nate Dern
Negin Farsad
Davy Rothbart

Journalism
Florangela Davila
Glenn Mott
Pete Theroux

Personal Essay/Memoir
Laura Barnett
Rebecca Bondor
Jill Eisenstadt
Elizabeth Eulberg
Lise Funderburg
Lauren Redniss
Eliot Schrefer

Persuasive Writing
Melinda Beck
Thom Duffy
David Shenk

Poetry
Holly Bass
Jen Benka
Brett Fletcher Laurer
Alison Granucci
Major Jackson
Laura Baudo Sillerman

Science Fiction / Fantasy
Maureen McQuerry
Kamran Pasha
Stephen Wallenfels

Senior Writing Portfolio
Eireann Corrigan
Kathryn Cullen-DuPont
Courtney Eldridge
Alaya Johnson
Bill Konigsberg
Elizabeth Lee Wurtzel

Short Story
Adam Berlin
Marjorie Celona
Andrew Conn
Edwidge Danticat
Myla Goldberg
Peter Quinn

EDITOR'S INTRODUCTION
Hannah Jones
2004 Portfolio Gold Medalist
Scholastic Art & Writing Awards

I edited *The Best Teen Writing* anthology once before, exactly ten years ago. I was seventeen at the time, it was the summer before I started college, and I took home boxes of writing on the subway. Now, I'm twenty-seven, all the student submissions are easily accessible through an online database, and I have never felt so close, emotionally, to dinosaurs.

Speaking of dinosaurs: There's only a small part of me that likes to think their bones are the reason why so many cultures, without methods of cross-communication, have dragons in their ancient mythologies, spontaneously arriving at the same monstrous conclusions based on these massive and inexplicable fossils. The other part of me still wants to believe the reason why so many cultures have dragons in their ancient mythologies is because dragons were, at some point, real.

That was a digression, possibly a non sequitur, definitely a laborious introduction to a metaphor, but here's the thing. There has to be a reason why so many of these student writers are capable of speaking to each other across time and distance without ever having met, holding up the same bones with the same dirty hands and deciding they'll tell their own stories. The results can be monstrous, sure—some arrive at dinosaurs and some at dragons—but the conversation is still ongoing.

I remember the pieces I read ten years ago the same way we remember fossils. You know, we've got the basic shape of the thing, shadowy, powerful, and frail. But the pieces I read yesterday aren't echoes. They're more like new flesh on old bones.

The best part is the moment when you realize that not only are they still talking, we're still listening. And reading and watching and responding, so it's a dialogue instead of a monologue—which is the one thing I *really* remember from when I was seventeen, before I became a dinosaur. That's when I was still collecting bones, asking myself if anyone was going to bother with excavating me someday, much less going to my museum.

The thing is, there's no collective voice; there's only a collection of voices. There are all these bones, and they've been put together to look like a dragon this time around because they were gathered and shaped by this particular dinosaur: me.

So, ultimately, you should probably choose to forget about me and forget about the bones. Once you've done that, you can decide for yourself what kind of museum this should be, and you can reshape that museum without ever changing what's on display there.

I still think of myself—incorrectly so—as the seventeen-year-old of ten years ago, as though the writing in this book is the writing of my peers. It's partly due to wishful thinking, more of that dragons-from-dinosaurs stuff I err in favor of, and partly a testament to the power of these voices. It's completely the point of these Awards. If you can stand beneath the fossils of a massive Brachiosaurus and think, "Yeah, dragons are possible, anything's possible," then you can be a part of what was left behind, because what was left behind has become a part of you.

Now read this book.

CHLOE CLOUD, *Nature Burn Nature*, Grade 11, Age 17. Maize Senior High School, Maize, KS. Bethany Janssen, *Educator*. 2014 Gold Medal

PORTFOLIO GOLD MEDALS

Graduating high school seniors may submit a portfolio of three to eight works for review by authors, educators, and literary professionals. Recipients of the Gold Medal Writing Portfolio receive a $10,000 scholarship.

Some of the writing selections have been excerpted. Go to **www.artandwriting.org/galleries** to read all of the work as it was submitted.

Morral

SHANNON DANIELS, Grade 12, Age 17. Stuyvesant High School,
New York, NY, Whitney Jacoby, *Educator*

I've stood on riverbanks.
I've known the Hudson,
who has hugged this urban playground of an island
from Whitehall to 220th, swallowed every bottle of soda
and half-eaten hot dog without hesitation, balls
its chubby fists and curses morning commuters
with sidewalks slick with tears.

I've seen the Mississippi,
who claims to have a muddy bosom that
turns all golden in the sunset,
but now I wonder if that glitter is just
dispersed oil.

Rosina collects the scales of fish
I cannot pronounce,
wears a braid trailing down her back
like her crescent of a Southern accent.
Her tribe members feel with their nets
for writhing treasures—sometimes three-eyed
or blind—in this poisoned womb.

I've learned that poetry is not a bandage,
that my words will not bring together
fragmented marshes or build stronger levees
or save struggling families from the next disaster.
But I will forever know Rosina's words—
when she told me that

the sweet plant "morral" can still grow out of this wetland,
polluted and damaged as it is.
The children love the taste, she tells me, and it's the first
time I mirror her beautiful, crooked smile.

I've known flowing rivers.
The rivers I've known flow through me.
I live in an ancient, dusky limbo between
the green-gray grandmother of the South
and the child of the North that I've returned to.
How badly I wish I could mend
this world.
This house of myself, this "an," is split irreparably,
roof ends curled toward overcast skies
the same white as the liquid absolution beneath me
breaking surface, open water,
slippery, inky mud.

Buried is what I've almost forgotten:
Rosina, the taste of "morral," and the glinting
promise of Louisiana at daybreak. Light chuckling
on the Hudson River's surface. Resilience.

Don't let these things
wash away.

Conjoined

NATHAN CUMMINGS, Grade 12, Age 18. Mercer Island High School, Mercer Island, WA, Creighton Laughary, *Educator*

This is the only thing that matters.

When I was three days old, doctors cut my brother off of my right side. As expected, he didn't survive the experience. They put him in a small box and gave him to my parents, who—not being much for pomp and circumstance—laid him to rest in our backyard. For all I know, he's still there. It doesn't matter. This is not his story. This is my story.

Funny how people have trouble telling the difference.

The term is conjoined twin, for the record; let's just get that out of the way. It doesn't help that my mom is from Thailand, of course. There are certain people who will never understand that that does not make me an actual, factual Siamese twin. Trust me, if you can make the connection, allow me to tell you it's been done before. Like on my first day of kindergarten: all the parents in the back, listening to their kids mumble their name and favorite color. Then I got up to speak. The teacher—a grey-haired, matronly type who'd apparently been briefed in advance—took one look at me and said to the whole room, "Will is a very special boy. He was born a Siamese twin." Instantly, the room went quiet; my mom got this furious gleam in her eye. Like, *I cannot believe you just said that.* The teacher seemed to sense she'd made some sort of faux pas but stubbornly decided to forge ahead. "Will," she said to me, her voice dripping with as much syrup as she could slather on, "what is your favorite color?"

I said red, and people automatically started trying to assign some sort of connection to my psychological profile, because there's no way a former conjoined twin could be interested in something as mundane as fire engines. One parent took a peek at my right arm, which has always been slightly shorter than my left, and he looked as if he wanted to pickle me in a jar.

School's gotten a little better over the years. Of course, I couldn't juggle quite as fast as other kids, but I was a mean shot at foosball, and I could freeze-tag with the best of them. It still goes around, though. People talk. They don't hate me for it. I wouldn't even say they pity me for it, which would be a million times worse than hate. But they identify me by it. Not Will, the bad juggler. Not Will, that kid with the dark hair and a bad sense of humor. Will, the kid with the scars.

Sometimes, when I'm lying in bed at night, I absently run my fingers up and down my right side. They are still there, impossibly faint outlines on the smooth textured plain of my skin. People used to look at them and wince, and for the life of me, I can't understand why. Sure, the process must have been painful, but so is getting your wisdom teeth out, and most people sure as hell remember that, whereas I don't have the slightest memory of being three days old and one-and-a-half people. These scars, I've grown up with them. To me they're just another part of my body. I run my fingers up and down, down and up, until I fade away into sleep.

The dreams began when I was ten years old. I would feel overwhelming darkness, a sense of pressure from all sides, and no air. I was incredibly thirsty; my skin seemed too dry. I tried to move, and my fingers crumbled into dust. That was usually when I woke up, gasping and sweating and not the least bit thirsty.

I was stupid enough to relate this to my psychologist when my parents signed me up—nothing's too good for our little malformed darling!—and he was over the moon. He dug into my medical file, turning up all sorts of information I didn't really want to know. Eventually, he dug up a picture of me when I was about a day old. I puked when I saw it. It must sound odd, puking at a picture of yourself, but beside me lay . . . something else. Scientists talk about the "uncanny valley" effect with robots: the closer something gets to normal, the more eerie and unnerving the remaining differences look. Well, the thing lying beside me . . . it wasn't whole, not even close. But I could still see hints of myself in it, in the hair, the curve of the forehead. I was looking at my personal uncanny valley, and it was a long way down to the bottom.

My shrink asked me, "Do you ever miss your brother?"

I said that it's kind of hard to miss someone who was in a catatonic state at birth and got cut off you before either of you could form full sentences.

He asked, "Do you ever hate him?"

That really set me off. What was to hate? Poor little bundle of nerves and giblets. He hadn't harmed anything in the world. He'd kind of gotten the short end of the stick, in fact.

"Do you ever feel like you were him?"

What a question. At that point, I was done talking. I screamed, and my parents scooped me up and placed me back in the car. The psychologist snapped a picture of me with his phone as I was being carried out. Prick.

So what if I have dreams about being buried alive. Are you

thinking that it's telepathic communication—that my brother's some sort of fetal zombie reaching out from beyond the grave? Bullshit. I had nightmares about being stuck in a shoebox, because for the longest time, when I imagined my brother, all I could think of is that it would be pretty awful to be stuck underground while I was out enjoying the sunshine.

Maybe that's it. I'm sure that would be the inevitable conclusion that the psychologist would draw. Simplified as much as possible, it would come out to something approaching survivor's guilt: I lived, and he died. Believe me, I've thought about this—and now, after sixteen years, I've finally come to terms with it.

Yes, I got lucky. Yes, I survived and my brother got the scalpel of doom. But here's the thing: If he was really my brother, I know he would have been happy for me. I imagine us having a conversation: me sitting in a folding chair, legs thoughtfully crossed, him lying in his little petri dish. "Take life by the horns, bro," he'd gargle at me in his squishy chipmunk voice. "Don't hold back. Go get 'em, for me." My imaginary little brother gives great advice. He'd have been a pretty cool guy, come to think of it. But then again, so am I.

And there you go. After so many bad dreams, I'm finally free as a bird, and the last thing I need is you throwing the same old paranoia back in my face. So get over the scars. Get over the photograph. Get over all your sick, twisted conspiracy theories, you nut. If I did, so can you. I am a normal person. Not a person and a half, not half of a person. I am whole. I am perfect.

Yeah, right. Like you're even listening to me right now. I know what people want to hear. So step up, folks, because here I am, the freak of nature, right next to the bearded lady and the limbless man.

We Don't Like You

JONATHAN GELERNTER, Grade 12, Age 17. ACES Educational Center for the Arts, New Haven, CT, Caroline Rosenstone, *Educator*

Todd was a sultan among slobs, who cultivated the filth of his apartment to such a horrific extent that his place had been declared unsafe for occupancy by the local building inspector. This was unfortunate, because his apartment was actually a converted barracks rented to him by my parents, and the time had finally come after ten years of dodged payments to evict him. We—my sister and I—arrived on the appointed day wearing full protective gear: Tyvek hazardous environment suits, nitrile gloves, respirators, and boots that we'd be willing to trash once we'd packed away Todd's things. Standing outside his apartment, I pulled on my respirator. "We have work to do," I told Rebecca, in my best Walter White growl.

Todd was waiting for us, his titanic swollen mass of a body barely contained by a stained V-neck and old pajama pants. He welcomed us into his apartment through the open screen door, and we headed down the hall to pack up his belongings.

Though conditions were not as bad as they had been when the police first came to visit Todd (since then, the bird corpses had been fished out of the half-inch-deep pool of turbid water in the living room), they were still pretty awful. Even through my respirator I could smell cat urine and decomposing sheet rock. The worn floorboards creaked flatulently underfoot. We'd decided to start in the bedroom, but getting to it was the kind of trek traditionally undertaken by a fellowship of hobbits and elves—we were forced to wade through a knee-deep swampy mass of old diet soda bottles and suspiciously abundant used Kleenex.

I had seen the police carrying wooden cases full of guns, black burnished metal in twisted arboreal towers, and enough ammunition to supply a small South American guerrilla army out of the apartment a few nights before; even so, when I walked around Todd's bed, I still sent handfuls of bullets skittering across the ground. As I heaved his bedside table into the U-Haul, the drawers slid open and out tumbled two porno DVDs. One was labeled "Young and Well-Developed," and pictured a big-breasted teenage blond girl pulling off her shirt. The other screamed, in manic red letters, "Sporty pussy inside!" I hastily stuffed the DVDs back in the drawer, hoping Todd would not appear at my shoulder to be embarrassed at my discovery, and wondered what exactly made a pussy sporty and why that would ever be appealing.

We emptied Todd's den of hundreds of old G.I. Joes, stuffing them into cardboard boxes, then used snow shovels and pitchforks to collect piles of trash and pour them into Heftys while Todd sat, paralyzed, on a living room loveseat. He finally groaned to his feet and lumbered down the hall to help me pack his movie collection into another box. "These are VHS tapes," he told me proudly. Todd would soon be unpacking them in his parents' apartment, where he would be moving into the basement.

"Yeah," I said. "I know."

Later, I showered for half an hour, washing off quarts of sweat. It was over ninety degrees outside that day, and those suits do not sit well. I don't know how meth cooks do it.

That afternoon, I reported to my first session of driver's ed. Mr. Bob, my new teacher, was a puzzling specimen—he looked not so much like a man who had just begun balding as a man who had just begun to sprout hair. An unruly grey halo hovered over his shiny scalp, and he wore a walrus moustache above his tumid lips that made me think of the Lorax.

"This class," he told us on his first day, "will not be like any other class you've ever taken. I like to have fun." He gazed at us in an awkward attempt at playfulness. "I like to joke around," he said. "I'm pretty sarcastic." Mr. Bob was a chronic self-describer, a man who had found that nobody had quite the mental image of him that he desired and so supplied it himself frequently and explicitly. "I try to make things fun," he continued. "I spice this course up a little bit. And now," he said, turning on a projector, "knowing your car! Let's start. Does anybody know what the wheels are for?"

Mr. Bob's opening monologue was interrupted when the door to the classroom swung open. A twenty-year-old boy with purple circles under his eyes walked in with his mother. He wore a T-shirt that read "Genius by birth, slacker by choice." I really hated that shirt.

"Sorry we're late," his mother said, and left. The young man—we'll call him Brian—sat down at a vacant desk.

"Get any sleep last night?" Mr. Bob asked.

"What?" the young man said.

"You look tired," Mr. Bob said, showcasing his trademark wit.

"Oh," Brian replied. "That's probably just my eczema."

Mr. Bob continued his lecture, and I, bored, tried to arrange my notes so that the acrostic would spell "D-E-A-T-H-I-S-N-E-

A-R." I saw the blond girl next to me shaking her head when she caught a glimpse of my work. When we were released for a five-minute break, I waited in line behind Brian for the water fountain. He made a funny sound when he drank, like instead of taking in water in the usual fashion, he was sucking it into his throat through the back of his neck. Put off, from then on I brought a water bottle to driver's ed.

That afternoon, the second round of Todd work began. Now that my sister and I had made his apartment habitable to mammals, we'd spend a long afternoon cleaning out the yard.

Todd had left behind an attempt at a gardening project—an iron framework of outdoor shelves that originally were intended to house plants. The project, like so many others, had been abandoned, as Todd was flattened by the slow-moving iceberg of his own malaise. Now Rebecca and I were tasked with destroying and carting away the rusted monstrosity. We took turns smashing it with a sledgehammer, the metal squeaking and tearing, and dragging away whatever we could to the dumpster. I sliced open my fingers on the jagged sheets of shelving and gave myself a nasty poison ivy rash. As I brought down the hammer with all of my negligible might, I put a silent pox on Todd, wherever he was.

"We don't like you!" I wanted to wail. "Can't you see!"

The next day, back in driver's ed, I took extensive notes on Mr. Bob's disquisition on the rules of right of way. "Nobody ever has the right of way," he'd say, over and over. "People yield the right of way, but nobody ever actually has it." But Mr. Bob was a well-rounded man, and, of course, had other things to share with us—things about his life, which he had devoted to more than just safe driving. It seemed that he had been an all-star baseball player in his youth, and a prodigious but effortless intellect.

"I was one of those kids," he told us, as the projector idled on with his drunk-driving PowerPoint behind him, "who never had to do anything. It drove my teachers crazy. I wouldn't study, and I'd do great on all the tests." He also claimed to own a collection of vintage cars that he kept in a climate-controlled facility in Florida, and to have a book in the works based on his experiences teaching driver's ed. When toward the end of class, he caught me reading the copy of *The Sirens of Titan* that I had stuffed in my textbook, he confiscated the book and recounted a story.

"I knew a guy in college," he said, "who could flip through a book like this for thirty seconds, and twenty minutes later he could tell you the whole plot by heart. He was a real genius. He was a CPA—do you know what that means?"

"Certified Pubic Accountant?" I offered. I noticed Mary—the disapproving blonde—wince as I said this.

"That's right," Mr. Bob said. "And he was a lawyer, and he got an M.D. Real genius. He could never put one over on me, though. It drove him crazy." Mr. Bob shook his head. If a Greek sculptor had captured the pose of a great teacher cautioning a wayward student, circa 200 A.D., the resulting limbless statue, consigned to a corner of the Met and labeled "The Folly of Youth," would look exactly like Mr. Bob.

"Yes," Mr. Bob continued. "He was brilliant. But at the age of thirty, he put a gun in his mouth and pulled the trigger. He left a note that said he had no more worlds left to conquer. That's right," Mr. Bob continued. "Let that be a lesson to you."

I wanted to protest—there were plenty of worlds left to conquer after accounting and the law. And he'd just described a good friend's death as if he were a cop in a movie. Instead, I nodded with feigned sympathy and waited for him to return my book.

He finally did, when class ended, and then I went outside with my classmates where we stood, aimlessly wishing for our rides to arrive.

"Pretty weird story, huh," I said to Mary, the blond girl from class. She grunted. An affirmative.

"I wonder if he knows how silly he sounds," I said.

"Maybe he wouldn't have to tell those stories if you weren't such an asshole," she said, and stalked off to a brown minivan that had just pulled up in front of us.

I was stuck there for some time before anyone came to pick me up. I leaned against a pillar in the parking lot and read, humming to myself a little composition I'd based on a classic by the Pixies:

"Where is my ride . . . Where is my ride . . . Wheeeeeere is my ride." Just as I was beginning to nod off, Mr. Bob appeared behind me. "Hey," he said. "What are you reading?"

I showed him the book he had confiscated forty minutes ago. "Oh," he said. "Is it good?"

"Yup."

He paused. "I wasn't actually mad at you today," he said. "Just joking around. You'll get used to me. Joking around." I nodded. "That's fine," I said.

He nodded, stood motionless for a few more seconds, then lumbered ataxically back to his car, whistling to himself, and I marveled at him. He was like Todd, sure never to hear people scream what I was sure we all wanted to scream, that "We don't like you!" And I thought how lucky he was, to never know what was in anyone else's head.

Sight Without Vision, Vision Without Sight

EMMA HASTINGS, Grade 12, Age 17. Thomas Jefferson High School of Science and Technology, Alexandria, VA, Jennifer Seavey, *Educator*

The vital organs go first. The second oxygen's no longer pumping through them, they become useless. So they have to be harvested while the heart's still being coaxed into beating and a ventilator's still funneling air into the lungs, obtained through solemn but pushy conversations in hospital waiting rooms while the family's wondering if "brain dead" means there's any chance for recovery.

It doesn't. Exactly the opposite, actually.

After the organs are out, the next time crunch comes. For kidneys, you have 48 to 72 hours to transplant, for livers, 18 to 24, and for hearts, 4 to 6. Thump-thump. Tick-tock.

Then there are the tissues. Those can be recovered after death, so they're easier to get, but even then there's a limited window before they've degraded too much to be useful. For skin, you can usually count on 24 hours being the maximum. Same with bones; those you can store for years before grafting. For corneas, you have to cut that time to a quarter. From the time the heart takes a licking and stops ticking, to get a technician on scene, to confirm the family's permission, to pronounce the body healthy enough to donate, to make the call to the tissue bank, to remove the thin slices of clear tissue and get them packed into wet ice—2-8°C, cold enough to preserve but not to freeze—you have 6 hours, no more.

Two weeks after that, the corneas must be transplanted, spliced onto some poor, near-blind bastard, restoring clear sight in a glorious realization of eyeball slicing and stitching and bloody, weeping sclera.

When people think about organ and tissue transplants, they usually picture the intrepid surgeon and the patient he recalls to life in a brilliant rebirth. Few spare thoughts for the guys like me, dividing up the dead to save the living. But someone has to do it. Six hours is a deceptively short time. Someone has to be ready, all hours of the day, to take the call, rush to the corpse, liberate the reusable pieces. That's me, the middle man of this messy miracle. It's just about as glamorous as it sounds.

* * *

When we finally slice some time out of our schedules to talk (on one of my on-call days, but that can't be helped), I see that April has a little bump on the back of her neck, right where the hair follicles give way to pale skin. It could be a harmless cyst, or it could be cancer. I reach up to touch it, and she slaps my hand away.

"Ow."

"You think now is a good time to try something?" she hisses.

"I wasn't. I was checking for lumps."

"Gross!" She swivels on the common room couch, scooting back to glare at me straight-on, crossing her arms defensively across her chest.

"Not there," I say, but that's actually not a bad idea. April doesn't seem the type for regular and rigorous self-examination, and statistics show that boyfriends and husbands are more likely to find breast cancer than the women themselves. "On your neck."

"What?" Her fingers tap across her skin, their cold tips giving her gooseflesh. In a few seconds they skitter over the benign bump/ticking time bomb of pain, tearful desperation, and death. She scowls. "That's nothing. You're just avoiding the subject."

The Subject. Always with The Subject. But which variant? The "You don't spend enough time with me," the "You're always distracted when we're together," or maybe the dreaded and all-encompassing, "You put everything in your life before me." I have 30 more lab hours and a thesis to complete, med schools to look at, a strict research regimen, and frankly, avoiding The Subject in all its incarnations sounded great. "You know, we could do that. Just forget about this, go out, actually make good use of the time we have for once."

Her eyes darken, her lips and skin pull taut, her eyebrows bunch and twist down like spasming flatworms trying to escape the scalpel. Her paleness and gauntness from too much time sequestered in the library digging out leather-bound 18th-century volumes snap into sharp focus. She looks like those pictures of demonic succubi that we saw in History of Medicine, the ones that doctors in the Middle Ages thought gave people nightmares.

I should have known that would have been too good to be true. "I was just kidding," I say. And in a way, I was kidding . . . myself. Ha. Haha.

The succubus face lightens, twists from one of wrath to something between contempt, condescension, and exaggerated exasperation. "Figures. We finally get time together, and you want to waste it clowning around like an ass."

"C'mon, I'm just—"

My pager goes off with the usual flickering blue light, vibrating, beep-beep combo on my belt, despite April's insistence that only douche bags clip things to their belts anymore. Douche bags and doctors, I say, and inevitably she shoots back, isn't that redundant, in a familiar rhythm, and we used to laugh as I kissed her before I left.

April's head shoots up as I stand, her eyes tracking me, filled with "please, just this once, don't go. . ." "It's at St. Francis," I say. "So I'll be back in a few hours. Probably three or four. We can talk more then."

"I have a poetry reading tonight."

I open my mouth, almost say, "Just skip it, then, you're the one who is insisting on these talks, not me," but then remember the succubus face and amend myself. "I probably won't make it."

"No kidding."

I pause with my hand on the common room doorknob. "I'm sure your stuff is great. I'm sorry."

"Aren't you going to be late?" April snaps, contempt dripping from her voice, and I want to shout back, "Yeah, actually, I am, and some poor suffering soul won't get their vision back, and if you miss your reading then the world will be for one night bereft of your elegant verses about how much a prick your boyfriend is."

But I manage to stop myself at "Yeah, actually," and step out of the door just in time to hear April mutter "douche bag," which I guess is a truncation of our old parting ritual. At least she hasn't forgotten. They say the opposite of love is indifference, not hate.

Home on the Range

JACK RAYSON, Grade 12, Age 18. University School of Nashville, Nashville, TN, Rob Travieso, *Educator*

I was the one who tied Suzy Winthrop to a post with the garden hose at the Cowboy's home base in the forest clearing, but I did it only because Amanda Bishop told me to. The Cowboys—seventh-, eighth-, and a few ninth-graders who didn't want to give up seniority yet—had already caught all the other fifth- and sixth-graders, all dressed in beaded necklaces and craft-store feathers, and kept them in a scared line over near the old iron ore processing factory that was falling away to bricks and wood and metal against the cold November gray sky that was a little bit soft. The Cowboys paced up and down the line of Indians, shoving them here and there and scowling like they'd seen Cowboys do in movies. We were two miles from the nearest grown-up.

"Assimilate!" Amanda said.

Suzy shook her head and her braided pigtails hit her eyes. Amanda pulled off Suzy's feather headband. Suzy had made it before we started, when all the other Indians were making their costumes in Lonnie Maynard's basement. It was a lovingly made headband, but Suzy had made it before she understood that this game of Cowboys and Indians was historically accurate. She hadn't known that she could never win, that she would lose, again and again, to our true God and our fake plastic repeating rifles. All she could've done was run and run and run until she was old enough to be a Cowboy, but instead she tripped on a root and fell headlong at our feet.

Amanda stepped on the headband and backhanded Suzy's mouth. I could tell it wasn't what Suzy had been expecting, but she'd moved here from some gentle town with a gentle school, so she was smart enough to be in the sixth grade here when she should've been in the fifth, and today she was the last Indian left. Amanda wasn't that good at hitting, not by my and Tommy's standard, but Suzy hadn't lived in this town that long, so she wasn't good at getting hit yet, and so her tears fell onto the quiet brown needles at her feet. The lines and triangles she'd drawn on her cheeks with a black marker trickled together into soft curves. Amanda took off her dress-up cowboy hat and spat in Suzy's face. Suzy looked at us, appalled and offended, like she wanted to protest our supposed cruelty or find a sympathizer among us, but Amanda cut her off.

"Assimilate," Amanda said, "you savage bitch!"

Suzy flinched and briefly searched along the line of her teammates, but they all wordlessly studied their shoes or stared at the sky, and I watched, satisfied, as the fight slithered out of Suzy's face.

"That wouldn't be a yes I see forming, would it?" Amanda said. For a moment Suzy didn't move, and then she shook her head. "Tommy," Amanda said.

Tommy didn't look up from the dirt. He fiddled with the long hair that grew from a freckle on his cheek. He kicked at a twig, and it scuttled a foot away and returned to rest. "I ain't gonna hit a girl," he said.

"What did you say?" Amanda said.

"I said I ain't gonna hit her."

Amanda turned and slapped Suzy again, only much harder this time. It was a good hit. Maybe the people in Denver heard the echo. Amanda is getting better at hitting. Suzy let out a short, painful cry and her mouth hung open. Her eyes got wide. She wasn't good at getting hit, not yet. She started crying harder and struggling against the green garden hose.

"Suzy," Tommy said, "just assimilate."

Suzy shook her head again and looked a bit defiant, glaring at us like her words would rise and leave us below, like we were the savages. A few Indians looked at Suzy, admired her silence. I couldn't wait to hit that girl. I couldn't stand her moving into our town and trying to smear her sunshine smile horseshit across the way it's always been. "Suzy," Tommy said. He was rubbing his hands together like he was washing them. His father's cowboy boots were too big for his feet, and they hurt his ankles when he walked, but Suzy hadn't lived in this town long enough to get good at getting hit.

"Hit her," Amanda said to Tommy.

"I ain't gonna hit her!"

"Fine, you pussy," Amanda said. She looked at the gray sky, toed a pebble away in her thought, and stroked the gentle red markings that her hand had left on our captive daughter of made-up tree religions, of the little ferns, the ideals we'd belonged to at her age but left behind for civilization and for the seventh grade. Amanda kissed Suzy lightly on the forehead.

"You're dead, Pocahontas," she said, almost lovingly, and allowed a moment of silence so that Suzy could redeem herself, drop her savage shackles, and go home for dinner and a hot shower and her mom's unquestioning love.

But Suzy said nothing, and I couldn't shake the feeling that all sounds that came near her suddenly died, painlessly and violently, shot through the temple with an arrow and posthumously scalped. All of a sudden, I didn't like standing. The games never lasted this long, they weren't supposed to last this long.

Then Amanda turned to me. "How about you, David?"

I looked at the Indian. The forest was still and cold and the sky was like wet cotton, poorly quilted. The first snowflake of the year drifted down from up there and passed by me before dampening the dirt on the ground. I walked over to the feral girl, helpless and tied up, and I couldn't help but smile. I was good at hitting, but I'd never hit a girl before. Sometimes I thought about hitting girls and their clean skin and thin muscles, and here stood a thing even less than a girl, an Indian who wanted to cut the balls off of Cowboys and Indians with her smiles and sort of skip walk through the forest, expecting the wilderness to welcome her with light song and an unending warmth that would wrap around her like a fur coat. She looked soft, like she didn't have any bones inside, and when she looked and saw me standing before her, her eyes became big and scared like a rabbit's when the rabbit's caught in a trap. I wanted to give her love, but that love was not something a savage could comprehend, not for anyone who could love so little and be so blind that she would not accept the love the Cowboys stood to give her without thinking or questioning. This wasn't her town, and I wouldn't let her take it from me.

So I punched Suzy across the jaw. The bones, the muscles, the tendons became a single softness that bowed and briefly died beneath my fist, my progress. Her teeth cut her lip. Blood leapt upon her chin. She started crying deeply and loudly. I guess she was sobbing or bawling. It was more than crying, and I hadn't ever witnessed something like it before, and it made me angry so I punched her in the stomach, and she went down to a whimper as she caught her short, weak breaths. Suzy's knees turned inwards, and she stood on the sides of her sneakers, the left one untied. There was no sound in the clearing save her frailty. I could smell someone's fireplace across the cold and empty air. The snowflakes began to fall faster. Suzy shivered.

The Balancing Act

HALEY LEE, Grade 12, Age 16. BASIS Scottsdale, Scottsdale, AZ, Hadley Ruggles, *Educator*

It began with a slice of cantaloupe. True, I managed to fake my way through dinner using a shallow serving spoon and the lip of my rice bowl as necessary crutches. But since clearing the other silverware from the table, my pretense of cutlery coordination had hastily started to deflate. Before I could gather my thoughts, the juicy truth tumbled out in melon form—

I didn't know how to hold chopsticks.

Thump.

The buzz of Chinese chitchat revved and then stalled. It was my first night with my host family on an NSLI-Yscholarship, a program that lists Mandarin proficiency and student ambassadorship as the end goals of a six-week stay in Hangzhou. To my horror, visions of hand-eye coordination had trounced those twin specters of fluency and diplomacy by the time my portion of fruit clunked against the wooden floorboards.

Zigzagging under the table and now trailing a sticky rivulet, the orange crescent resembled too closely the arc of a mocking smile. I couldn't help grinning in response, feeling helpless and a little ridiculous crouched on my knees. It was my host father who, after I collected myself and my dignity, spoke. "Do you want us to teach you how to use them?" He pointed to the instruments of my destruction, the chopsticks resting innocently against the broad-brimmed dessert platter.

Presented with this question now, "yes" seems like the obvious reply. At the time, I hesitated before answering. During childhood meals, I vacillated regularly between using chopsticks and a fork. The former promised dexterity and grace, the type of swanlike agility detailed by Amy Tan and wielded by Mulan. But in the end, the precision demanded by chopsticks proved too frustrating for me, and so the pair's pronged American counterpart, commanding in ease and in gleam, won my young heart.

Nobody judged me for choosing between utensils. In fact, at annual New Year's Eve dinners with my dad's Chinese family, my grandma has more than once slid me a fork after watching oysters come back to life between my trembling chopsticks. My nebulous "Whasian" (half white, half Asian) status served as a ready-made excuse for my fumbling. So before my host father broached the subject, I lived for years believing my silverware scrimmages lay in the past. While I cannot claim to know what force compelled me to nod in response to his offer, I do attribute my semi-mastery of chopsticks to his advice:

"Relax your hand. The rest will come with practice." My fingers slackened. I exhaled, relieved.

As a child, I let the fork triumph at chopsticks' expense. I reasoned seeking refuge in my mom's American influence would lead to a cleaner daily existence—fewer inquiries about the contents of my lunch box if I toted a ham-and-Swiss sandwich instead of sweet pork buns; fewer raised eyebrows when I told stories if I dubbed my grandma "Nana" instead of "Ngin Ngin." But as my grip loosened, I began to see that where I had staged a duel, there was no need for a dichotomy in the first place. My hands needed a lesson in pliability, but so did my mind.

Today, lowering my own pair of chopsticks into a bowl of instant ramen, I know that my host father was right: I must pursue the challenge of embracing silverware options and, ultimately, cultures. Being half Chinese doesn't justify hiding behind half commitments. It took a plunging cantaloupe wedge to dislodge my inertia, but since returning home I have successfully pinned tofu with chopsticks; I have started conversing with my grandma in Mandarin; I have begun to delve into literature on modern China. Although still a long way from achieving student statesmanship, I am enjoying savoring my fusion heritage. There is room for both a fork and chopsticks on my plate. And sometimes, I've learned, it's more fun to make a mess.

What I Know About River Fallwell

JACKSON TRICE, Grade 12, Age 17. South Carolina Governor's School for the Arts and Humanities, Greenville, SC, Scott Gould, *Educator*

Linnie Fallwell ate her twin. Everybody knows it, but she doesn't mind telling you twice. We're eating bologna sandwiches, Linnie and I. Swatting flies and scratching mosquito bites on our ankles. Linnie's telling me how it is. She's going, "Being a twin comes with certain compromises." It's the summer before high school, and we haven't outgrown playing barefoot in the Big Fallwell Yard, or drinking out of juice boxes.

Linnie stuffs some bologna in her mouth. She isn't eating white bread because she read somewhere that it kills you. (I'm eating her white bread. I'm saying we're all dying sooner or later.) I say, "Yeah, and?"

"And," she says, "I don't compromise. I'm smart enough to know you gotta do it on your own. Smart enough to know you gotta nip compromise in the bud, if you ever want to do something miraculous." She takes another bite of bologna, as if to say, "It's just that simple."

Linnie's backyard is just one big hill. The house sits on top of it. Big Fallwell Hill, we all call it. It levels out to grass and then mud and then River Fallwell. The largest river in all of Briner County, on account of being the only one. Don't ask why we don't call it Fallwell River, because we'll punch you in the mouth. The whole county, collectively. It's River Fallwell, and that's the end of it.

Near the bottom of the hill (the part where it's all grass and not yet mud) sits a big van humming along with the bugs' hymnal of summer. Six men with northern accents are setting up flashbulbs and fancy cameras, and telling Mr. and Mrs. Fallwell to "Sit up nice and straight. That's it."

"What about your brothers then?" I ask. "You calling them stupid for both being born?"

"Yes. I've got two theories."

"Never heard that one before," I say. Linnie always has a theory, but they're just plain ideas. Don't let anybody tell you different.

"Shut up, Opal, I ain't finished talking. My first theory is this: Silas tried to eat Simon, but he got a little mixed up. I chose Silas because everyone knows he's dumber than Simon. Simon would've done the job right."

"And your second theory?" I peel the crust off each slice of bread delicately so they stay intact. I hold them like snakes in my hand.

"They got too scared of the world and decided they couldn't live without each other."

"Which do you prefer?" I ask.

Linnie looks down at the cameramen with the northern accents and her parents and her brothers sitting all proper. "The first one. I like to give people the benefit of the doubt."

* * *

Here's what I know: Linnie Fallwell has gone off the deep end. By the time I arrive at her house, she's telling boys she knows secret places where they could both go. She's sweating, even though the night has taken most of the heat with it. When she opens the door to let me in, she screams, "Opie!" and hugs me. She smells like someone I don't know. The music is too loud for me to tell her this. Everyone's moving and yelling and dancing, and I get elbowed in the ribs by a stranger before I can ask her what the hell is going on.

* * *

Here's what I know: River Fallwell runs through Briner County like a nosebleed. Mrs. Hotchkiss's dog once drank the water in it and died. It ain't pretty or useful. It just trickles through the county, getting gifts from the sewers, flooding when it rains too hard during thunderstorms. We keep it like a bruise. Sometimes you gotta tamper with it and feel the ache just to know you're alive. Every once in a while, some poor dead girl will show up floating in the river basin. Every once in a while, some scientist will test the waters and tell us to evacuate. Every once in a while, some drunk will drive their car into its depths, but for the most part, we leave it alone. For the most part, we try and stay away from it, thinking maybe if we don't mess with it, it'll resolve itself. Dry up and leave us be.

The Fallwells can't run from it. It runs toward them. Back when old Fallwell Sr. died of an exploding appendix, the river was given to Mr. Fallwell Jr. He married some girl from outside Briner named Lady. Called her his Lady Fallwell. They got pregnant with twins, and that's where it all starts, with Baby A and Baby B. Baby A and Baby B sat all nice for a while, until Baby A decided it was done with compromising, and swallowed Baby B whole. Linnie A. Fallwell's claimed she's better than the rest of us ever since.

Then there was the spring three years later, where Mrs. Fallwell got sick for seven months, and Linnie spent most of her time at my house, on account of our mothers' being close. Everyone's close in Briner. When Mrs. Fallwell got better, all the news vans came, because a miracle had happened. Linnie's twin brothers Silas and Simon had been born two months early and stuck together. They had one heart, two arms, two legs.

The scientists tried to tell them it was the water. Preacher Wilson tried to tell them it was their own curse. That river's stream was downright unholy, and now God was reminding them who's boss. The Fallwells ignored all this—they were too busy getting money from every newspaper to have their faces on the cover. The hum of vans full of men with northern accents has kept them distracted ever since.

* * *

The house is drowning in beer and Coke. Everyone's spilling everything, and since they don't have to clean it up, they don't care. The living room is a sea of elbows, just trying to get by, one big "excuse me, pardon me." At 8:56, Linnie pulls the cable out of the stereo and the room stops thumping. At 8:57, Linnie turns off the lights. People start screaming, because that's what teenagers do when you turn off all their lights. Among other things. Linnie goes, "Oh, shut the hell up." The room goes silent. She says, "Y'all know what to do."

* * *

Silas and Simon are having their second birthday party when Mrs. Fallwell forgets her lighter in the car. Linnie and I are both five. Gangly things, with hair we weren't worried about always fixing just yet, and noses a size too big for our faces. We're barefoot. The party is a barbecue on top of Big Fallwell Hill, and the children of the neighborhood slide down it. Briner's very own amusement park—a little mud and altitude. The smell of hamburgers rises and falls over us.

"Linnie, watch the boys," Lady Fallwell says, and Linnie nods.

"Okay, you grab Silas's hand, and I'll grab Simon's," Linnie whispers after her mother is out of sight.

"What?" I ask. "Why?"

"Shh, just do what I say," she whispers. "We don't have much time." That's how it is. Linnie tells me what to do, and I listen.

"Okay," she says, after I grab hold of Silas's hand. "One . . . two . . . three. Pull!"

"Linnie!" I let go of the boy's hand. "You can't do that! You can't just pull them apart."

"That's what everyone says," Linnie goes. "But I'm sure nobody's ever tried."

"Well, I ain't helping you with this one," I say.

"Fine." Linnie grabs hold of both her brother's necks—one in each hand, and begins to pull. The boys start crying. Choking, little gagging noises.

"Linnie, stop! Stop it!" I yell.

"Will you quiet down?" Linnie goes, but she gets stopped short by the sight of her mother standing over us.

"Linnie A. Fallwell, just what in the hell do you think you're doing?" Linnie lets go. Mrs. Fallwell picks the twins up and settles them on her hip. She points to the house. "Go," she says. Terse and brimming with an anger I don't want to stick around to see.

"And don't expect me to bring you a slice of cake later. You just go on inside that house and stay there. Understand?"

"Yes," says Linnie, real soft. Silas wipes the tears off his face and then off his brother's. Simon stares at me with googly blue eyes. I wonder where his head wanders off to.

"Excuse me, I don't think I heard you," Lady Fallwell says.

"Yes, ma'am," Linnie says, as if she's got a frog in her throat.

Oranges

HANEL BAVEJA, Grade 12, Age 17. Huron High School, Ann Arbor, MI,
Sean Eldon, *Educator*

After, I could never bear to feel the rinds—like
freckled paper, lined with something rotting.

I had never liked them anyway—the raw brace of
blood, the pinpricked dimples, the tide of deflation.

After, I could not stop dreaming about her small hands.
I loathed every infant I saw, every woman who was not

you. The ways in which we knew, and didn't. After, I sat
in a dark room and stared down: a picture of a monarch

butterfly, a yellow balloon, half a jagged stick of citrus gum.
All neon, all glowing. After, the damp silence that grew like

night. Grocery stores became war zones. I still dream about
Charleston, about the verandah, that summer, your thumbs

swiftly cleaving the peels as smoothly as anything your belly
had ever required. The snap of skin, the cold release that

followed like a long winter. After, the understanding we held
between us, as plump as an orange, as hollow as its peel.

JOHN VAILE, *The Animal Within*, Grade 10, Age 16.
Archmere Academy, Claymont, DE. Jody Hoffman,
Educator. 2014 American Visions Medal

GOLD, SILVER, AMERICAN VOICES, AND CREATIVE CONCEPT AWARDS

Students in grades 7–12 may submit works in 11 writing categories. This year more than 3,400 Regional Award–winning writing submissions were reviewed by authors, educators, and literary professionals. Gold, Silver, and American Voices medals were awarded to works that demonstrated originality, technical skill, and emergence of a personal voice.

Creative Concept Awards recognize works that deal with tolerance (Gedenk Award for Tolerance); immigration and identity (Creativity & Citizenship).

Some of the writing selections have been excerpted. Go to **www.artandwriting.org/galleries** to read all of the work as it was submitted.

Nine Letter's War

EMMA HENSON, Grade 11, Age 16. Out-of-Door Academy,
Sarasota, FL, Andrew Lemieux, *Educator*

I've written you nine letters in scarlet-blood ink, words upon paper like veins beneath one weak wrist or arteries curving up the marble column of a proud neck.

I

I don't like half of the things you do to me, but I do not say a word, because I figure you won't be alive as long as I will. I try not to feel like we are shivering, because the Fates made the tapestry of your life far too short to reach my toes, and you are so much taller than me.

II

I have never learned to stop looking at you with words when all you ever do is speak to me in tongues. It's fuckery, and I am sorry.

III

I know now asking promises that involve you living longer is selfish of me. I don't want you to stay, as much as I simply don't want to feel beholden to your sadness. I suffer you like a millstone tied to my neck, the rope cutting into the bruises left from your callous and calloused words, your indefinable tendency toward the morose.

IV

I feel like I am always having a ménage-a-trios with your melancholia, but I'm afraid of being outnumbered. I've told you that, and you do not seem to remember.

V

The notebook you see me carrying around isn't of places that are too beautiful to look at only once, I'm not such an idealist. It's filled with notes I take whenever I'm around you; half sentences like his fingernails have white suns rising above his cuticles. They're for your eulogy, the piece I know I'll have to write. You understand this, you're too smart not to, but you've yet to say a word.

VI

When you introduce me to your friends, and one of them grabs my hand in both of his like Byzantines, drawing his palms up my forearm as if he were checking for swords in an ancient bazaar, I hate as his thumbs start searching for scars. Even more than that, I loathe that he seems surprised you would bring someone who does not wear their pain there. I despise feeling like the light within me hurts the darkness you foster.

VII

I feel like I have been trying to burn you for years, but every time I go to wipe the ash from my hands, I find them full and trembling. They are shaking, half-containing the smoldering embers of your minstrel's soul, pieces of you falling between my fingers like old, lost promises.

VIII

I say to take some aspirin and drink black coffee when you called me drunk on dark molasses rum. You tell me that you're a convert to whichever church I am the matriarch of, and I remind you that you've always been an atheist. No one can make gods of people, not any more than you're capable of believing in a deity. I should have told you that.

IX

My mother should have warned me to never trust someone who has eyes as transient as yours; vacant in the same exhalation as they turn bright and empty like quicksilver or hellfire. She should have told me that people cut from your cloth fuck like Achilles and leave like Odysseus. But we never seem to leave each other, only part and crash together again as if we are deep-ocean waves. Just like you are sad and I am verbose, it simply is.

The stationery is ivory, musty, old, organic, rotting. All nine of the envelopes are sitting in the bottom of my desk drawer, craving my iron lamp's light after many months of darkness.

Though Rome has fallen, it is hard to leave. Selah.

Lessons My Mother Taught Me

CAROLINE TSAI, Grade 10, Age 15. Canterbury School, Fort Wayne, IN, Alice Hancock, *Educator*

Barbie *noun* \\'bahr • bee\\ 1. According to a study by the University Central Hospital in Helsinki, Finland, Barbie lacks the 17 to 22 percent body fat required for a woman to menstruate. Slumber Party Barbie, who made her debut in 1965, came with a book titled *How to Lose Weight*—one of its more succinct but pertinent tips was "Don't eat." 2. Dear Pam, thanks for the lovely gift, but she really doesn't need Barbies. Do you happen to have that gift receipt?

fat *adjective* \\'fat\\ 1. The word implied by Dr. Joseph when I step on the scale in the stark white lights of Room 11; the circled dot in ballpoint pen on a red graph. 2. Slipped into a giggle as you pinch my waist; you meant nothing, I heard you too clearly. 3. Tale recounted from the fourth-grade bathroom, PE. "She doesn't even have boobs. The bra is just to hold in the fat."

panic *noun* \\'pa • nik\\ 1. My brother was born in 2003 and came home healthy. Three days later, he was back in the hospital room. Tubes everywhere. He didn't look human. An unanswered question haunted all of us. "Something's wrong, he's not breathing." I can still hear you gasping. 2. The glinting of street lights on pavement where it had recently rained; you stormed out in tears and shut the front door. I was afraid you wouldn't come back. 3. One of my best-kept secrets. It lurks in my closet.

Gilmore Girls *TV show* \'gil • mohr • gerls\ 1. Saturday morning. I have the potato chips and you make smoothies. You are on call, you have to do surgery, but you are never, ever too busy for this. 2. Carole King re-recorded "Where You Lead" for the popular 2000s television series *Gilmore Girls* with her daughter, Louise Goffin. The song was used as the series' theme song. 3. "Why does Rory leave her mom? Doesn't she love her?" "Maybe Rory grew up. Maybe Rory knows it's time to move on."

bra *noun* \'brä\ 1. Held up in front of my shirt in front of a crowded Target. "Does this one fit?" 2. See *fat*, third definition. 3. Second tale recounted from the fourth-grade bathroom, PE. "You're a fourth-grader! Why aren't you wearing a bra?" 4. The strange phobia I had when I was eight. The thought of those alien beings setting up camp on my chest sent me to tears. "Boobs! Boobs!" you cowered. "Headline: Boobs!"

camp *noun* \'kamp\ 1. 1979. Somewhere in Michigan, you forget about responsibilities. Two weeks feels like two minutes. You love it here. 2. "So you're homesick!" reads the sign on the back of the toilet stall door cheerfully, next to graffiti reading *call Janice for a good time.* "Call your mom! She'll make you feel better!" Later, I do. My brother yells in the background. Your voice on the other end of the phone makes my stomach drop. How many days left again? 3. 2009. Somewhere in Michigan, I am waiting for someone to pick me up. Two weeks feels like ten years. I hate it here.

airport *noun* \'er • port\ 1. 1998. Logan International. You wait with me, a bundle of blankets in your arms. Dad steps off the plane and sees you. "So this is her, eh? Can't believe I missed it." "Welcome home." 2. 2008. Chicago O'Hare. We descend the escalator. You're holding the suitcase with wheels, because I don't know how to push the handle down. "Maybe this is where we'll pick you up when you come home from college. You think you'll miss us?" 3. 2013. Indianapolis International. My luggage weighs my shoulder down. I see you in Baggage Claim. You smile. "Welcome home."

The Beatles *band* \the • bee • tels\ 1. The Beatles made great music together. We listen on road trips. You sing the harmony, because it's harder and you like a challenge. They broke up in 1970. You remember crying. They made great music together. 2. When you were little, you tried to record "Hello Goodbye" from the radio and always missed the beginning. Damn it. 3. "Daddy, our baby's gone / Why would she treat us so thoughtlessly? / How could she do this to me?"—"She's Leaving Home" by the Beatles (1967)

pretty *adjective* \'pri • tee\ 1. "This, this is about my own someday daughter. When you approach me, already stung-stayed with insecurity, begging, 'Mom, will I be pretty? Will I be pretty?' I will wipe that question from your mouth like cheap lipstick and answer, "No! The word pretty is unworthy of everything you will be, and no child of mine will be contained in five letters. You will be pretty intelligent, pretty creative, pretty amazing. But you will never be merely 'pretty.'"—Katie Makkai, "Pretty," 2002 National Poetry Slam. 2. You ask if I had to choose, would I be smart or pretty? I break the rules: both.

college *noun* \'kä • lij\ 1. "What's wrong?" The light clicks on and I am five years old, tucked in the covers with glassy eyes. "I don't want to go away to college." "Why not?" "I'm scared. And I'll miss your chocolate brownies," I say. You chuckle. "I guess you'd better get all the chocolate brownies you can get while you're here then." 2. You bought me a Princess Jasmine lamp and mirror and told me to keep it for my dorm. I think you didn't like the idea of me growing up.

Inside Phnom Penh

FRANCESCA PARIS, Grade 12, Age 17. Head-Royce School, Oakland, CA, Andy Spear, *Educator*

Outside the plane window, lights spread out like crooked tree branches across the surface of the continent. One river of light snakes away from us, growing dimmer as it probes its way into the blackness of the night. The sun slipped across the edge of the world almost an hour ago, and for the first time since we took off from SFO a day ago, we are swallowed whole by the night.

Peter has been sleeping on my shoulder since we crossed over Vietnam. Clementine is also fast asleep. Across the aisle, Sara, our teacher and guardian, is struggling to keep her eyes open. Cambodia looms on the horizon, not even an hour away.

"Does this qualify as a monsoon?" Clementine wants to know when we duck inside Sara's hotel room, away from the rest of the group, drenched to the bone and almost cold for the first time since we arrived. The country is on the brink of wet season, and it shows. Phnom Penh is under siege by the rain.

"Sure." Sara's attention is on her journal, and I watch as her steady hand slides across the book, dark ink slowly devouring the blank page. Peter is on his feet in an instant, rushing to join Clementine at the window, palms against the cool glass. He motions for me to join them, so I do.

"Isn't that the girl who was trying to sell us bracelets?" We watch a tiny, black-haired girl drag a heavy basket across the street, toward the cover of an awning of the bar across the street. In the distance, the sharp, golden tips of the Royal Palace jut out above dilapidated buildings. The faint clatter of construction carries on. A man on a bicycle crosses the asphalt below us. He makes no effort to shelter himself from the storm. A motorcycle driver pulling a rickety cart stops at the side of the road to pull a tarp over his cargo. We see all of this unfold from the hard, wooden window ledge, the room silent except for the soft whisper of Sara's pen on paper.

When we stop at Pour un Sourire d'Enfant, a nonprofit school started two decades ago by a French couple, our trip leader surprises us with manicures. For everyone. After a volunteer shows us around, detaching tiny children in uniforms from her legs while they gape at us, someone leads us to the beauty school. Inside, fans chase away the persistent heat, and I wipe away drying sweat from the back of my neck. Beside me, Peter sits in a chair in front of a large mirror looking vaguely uncomfortable, until one student offers to wash his hair instead. The quiet girl who has begun to scrub my fingernails looks up at me, smiles almost guiltily, and assures me that she is the best of all her peers. Later, when I compare the silver sheen of my nails to Clementine's pink, I can only agree.

We descend back into the younger children's sector of the school to eat lunch with them. Peter's hair is dry by the time we manage to say goodbye to all the students. One girl pulls at my shirt as I turn away. She holds up the Christmas card that I had pulled out earlier, to show her pictures of my family. I take it back and thank her, but she pulls at me again, so I bend down to her level.

"My name is Seyha," she repeats in faltering English for the third time.

"Yes," I tell her. "And you're eleven years old." I remember this because before she told me, I had believed she was seven, maybe eight. Not eleven. Not the same age as my own sister. "I have to go now." With a final hug, she consents. I catch up to Peter. The sharp air-conditioning hits us as soon as we step on the bus.

I watch Seyha through the window as we leave. Her attention is already elsewhere. She pulls on a friend's arm, then disappears from view entirely.

Where the morning is full of smiles and manicures, the afternoon swelters with silence.

The smell at Choeung Ek, better known to the world as the killing fields, isn't death—it's been three-and-a-half decades, and the bones have been removed and cleaned. The bones have been piled up in the glass monument at the center of the compound, and the skulls glisten in the sun. There have been no rotting remains of humans here for many years. So the smell isn't decomposing bodies. It's something else entirely, strong but, so far, undefinable.

A group of Cambodian girls and boys waits in front of us at the ticket line. One of them says something and the rest burst into laughter. I search their faces as we enter through the gates and keep coming back to one girl, the way her eyes constantly flit between the teacher and the boy with a mop of dark hair.

Tall blades of grass sprout out of the dirt-covered mass graves like a tiny army, perfectly still in the humid, motionless air. Wooden poles rise from the ground, topped by chipped loudspeakers that once upon a time played the Khmer Rouge's national anthem so loudly that no one outside of the compound could hear a thing. A large sign reads: 86 mass graves. 8,985 victims.

Around one of the largest graves, from which they have dug up the corpses of more than one hundred women and children, wooden fence posts are ringed with colorful hair bands and decorative bracelets. I hesitate here for a minute longer than the rest of the group, and only Sara sees me pull the brown hair band that Clementine had lent me that morning out of my hair and stretch it around a post. She says nothing, just holds out another elastic, and I twist my hair back up again as we rejoin the group.

As we leave, I break a stem beneath my shoe, and I realize what the smell is. Flowers. With the return of the rain, they have begun to spring from the graves like colorful carpets. I turn to look for Sara, for Peter or Clementine, to tell them, but they've boarded the bus already. Another of our chaperones appears next to me and tells me to hurry up, so I do, and by the time I'm sitting next to Peter again, chugging a bottle of water from the mini-freezer, I've already forgotten it.

The heat is less overwhelming at S21, where we can duck into the buildings and out of the sun. The building complex is a museum now: Tuol Sleng Genocide Museum. Genocide. A word, Peter had reminded me earlier that day, that didn't even exist in its modern capacity until 1943. Here, on the site of a former high school, the Khmer Rouge held more than 17,000 academics, monks, engineers, former government officials, and, as dictator Pol Pot grew more paranoid, Khmer Rouge soldiers and leaders.

Our guide tells us that only some of the prisoners were killed here; others were shipped to Cheoung Ek in trucks. Either way, by the end of the Khmer Rouge's regime in 1979, there were only twelve survivors.

Peter and I slip away from the group and up a flight of stairs. From the middle level, we can see the entire courtyard, palm trees sprouting from the ground and brightly colored birds scattered along the broken tiles. Walking through the rooms, we look at the faces in silence. The prison staff photographed every single person who passed through the facility, and their black-and-white portraits now line the walls. The faces are sometimes scarred, sometimes emaciated, always emotionless.

When the faces begin to blur into one, we slip back into the group as if we were never gone.

At Tiny Toons the next morning, they expect us to dance. The inner city nonprofit has pulled children off the street and taught them everything from English to mathematics to hip-hop dance. I don't doubt the value of the institution, but I don't dance. When Sara isn't watching, I slip out the backdoor, bare feet on the cracked concrete ground, a soft hum of noise emerging as the loud music disappears. Water spreads through the fissures in the ground like veins. I ask for the bathroom, and a boy points me across the courtyard.

The floors of this building are spotless, so I stop at the entrance and look as I dry my feet on the rug. Computers line one of the walls, and books the other. Children work and play in an orderly chaos reminiscent of one of our classrooms back home. When I finally find the bathroom, then exit, there is a girl waiting, hands behind her back, dark eyes trained on me.

"Choum reap souar," I tell her, the words spilling ungracefully from my tongue. It is the formal hello in Cambodian, and I imagine I sound about as sophisticated as a toddler speaking for the first time to her. She laughs, not unkindly.

"Hello," she says. She's a foot shorter than me, but she is sixteen—my age. After we've exchanged introductions, a gleam of silver from her neck catches my eye. She is wearing a pendant of a ballerina, one leg bent in a perfect loop.

"I like your necklace," I tell her, and I think she understands, because she starts smiling, then runs off. I linger for a moment to browse the books on the shelf, all English childrens' books, from Dr. Seuss to Shel Silverstein. Books that I grew up with.

When I am halfway across the courtyard, returning to the first building, the girl catches up with me, only now her neck is bare, and the necklace lies coiled in her palm. She offers it to me, and my protests are in vain. As it becomes clear that she won't take no for an answer, I nod.

"Okay," I say, but my hands move up to the clasp of my own necklace: a metal shark-tooth painted gold that couldn't have cost more than ten dollars. My necklace, which might have been made in this very country. I think about that as I undo the clasp and hold it out for her: maybe this necklace is coming home. We tie the necklaces around each other's necks, first hers, then mine.

Unconfined

JADE YOUNG, Grade 8, Age 13. Lakeside Middle School,
Seattle, WA, Susie Mortensen, *Educator*

Shadows and Salty Air

Jade. A shade-loving plant, a pretty color and a coveted stone.
But my name Jade is more than that. It is the serenity of a
quiet forest nook, where many a quiet soul has found solace
from all the problems of the world. It is the dark color of the
evergreens that overlook this shady pool and the sweet aroma
of pine that settles in the air like a perfume. It is the gentle
kiss of sunlight through a canopy of leaves, the quiet rustling
of the wind through the trees, the atmosphere of contemplation that surrounds someone ruminating by the pond.

Jade. Sometimes they say it as if they do not feel the underlying power of the name, as if the person who belongs to
it is delicate, gentle, nothing more. It is as if all they see is
the shady nook, when in fact the name buzzes with power, vibrant coral, vivid magentas and fiery oranges that make up the
brightest shades of the world. It is the unexpected side of the
name Jade, which so often conveys cool shades of green. It is
the sweet smell of salt on the wind, the crystal-clear water lap-
ping away at the brightly shining sand. It is the wild, foaming
waves of the ocean, and that is who I am. Some days my tem-

pestuous waves of feelings beat furiously down upon anyone who dares to come within the reach of their wrath, but other days my emotions lie placid and smooth, watching everyone, observing everything.

The two sides of Jade show the Janus-faced natures of my name. The peaceful corner of the forest is a happy place. Sometimes I like to pull myself out of the moment and go to this private sunny glade where all peace is preserved for eternity, but other times I rush into something like dashing into the foamy white arms of the waves—head-on and reckless. Unconfined, the shadows and the salty air, are me.

Neverland

Sophia. I can't remember when she moved into the other corner house at the very end of the street. I don't remember the first time we met, or how, or when I began to know her. Maybe it was one of those little-kid things, where you meet someone and by the end of the day you've declared your everlasting friendship. Or maybe there was a tentative greeting forced into a connection by our sisters' many sports they played together. All I know is that my first memory of Sophia is one of knowing her.

Over the years we grew to be friends. We acted out Cinderella and Snow White in her backyard, making our sisters play the dwarves or ugly stepsisters. During my obsession with Italian names, we were poor Italian street-sweepers who slept in the basement of a gondola (we hadn't quite thought the whole concept through). She came over when the '08 snowstorm forced us to cancel our gingerbread party, leaving our family with an excess 120 gingerbread cookies and a dozen candy bags. That day we were robbers; stealing the sweets away, then later we put together a thousand-piece puzzle. That year we also ditched the Little Mermaid reenactments and rode off on our motorcycles. We thoroughly annoyed both our moms by vroom-vrooming through the house after M (resident evil genius, also known as my terrified shih tzu). At some point we left the motorcycles behind and would draw, paint, go gallivanting around the neighborhood, and chatter about our lives together as we ran so many unsuccessful lemonade stands.

As we got older, we gossiped, we complained, we watched movies. We talked about things that we couldn't talk about with our school friends, like how you're crushing on your friend's crush, or how much that one girl annoys you. We blasted music, painted our nails, and made dirty references over our sisters' heads. We're friends, we have private jokes, and we can give each other the look that means "I'm going to lie us out of this situation, so just go along with it."

We've gone on camping, skiing, hiking trips together, celebrated Thanksgiving together, and marched up and down the street singing at the top of our lungs until a grouchy neighbor shut us down. There are so many memories and stories that bond us together. We could talk about things that we didn't want to discuss with anyone else: what it felt like to switch schools, mean girls, the ups and downs and surprises of sex ed, and why on earth would anyone want to get their legs waxed?

I don't see Sophia as much anymore, but it doesn't matter, because we have a deep connection that extends past time. We bonded over Neverland, Hogwarts, and eventually Forks, Washington; in other words, we bonded over growing up.

Imperfect Angel

The words come often. The compliments. Pretty, smart, funny. It makes me happy to hear them. But one day I realize that the people who tell you these things sometimes speak with honeyed tongues.

"You're totally awesome," she says with a grin. I smile, my face lighting up with the elation of being complimented. I go home and tell Mom I have a new friend and that I think we will be best friends.

The next day you hear her at the lockers.

"Who's in your group?" her friend asks casually.

She pauses, thinking, and rattles off about ten names. I wait to hear my name, as we are in the same group, but it never appears.

"That's it?" her friend asks. "My group has sixteen people in it."

"Well, you know," she replies, with a meaningful look. "It's like, everyone important."

Her words snap something deep inside of me. I make a silent retreat to the bathroom before they see me standing, shattered, behind them. Then I lock myself inside the stall and silently let the tears gush. All year struggling to fit in, and I still am not the same, still don't belong. My mind takes over you, filling me with ugly words, ugly feelings. You thought she was your friend? Ha! You're not the same as her. A tear gently caresses my cheekbone before sliding into the corner of my mouth. But why? Is she better than me? Confused, emotional thoughts ricochet around my head randomly, popcorn exploding in a machine. Middle school is hard, much harder than I ever expected.

The warm tears leave traces on my sweater. I want nothing more than to be at home, safe and warm, but I know I can't stay locked up forever in this dirty, claustrophobic bathroom stall.

I run to my locker and grab my jacket. Zip it all the way up, hide the tear marks and keep safe and warm inside the fleecy coat. The rain outside feels good today. It gives me an excuse to keep my head down.

I press my forehead to the cool bus window and tell myself not to cry. Get off the bus but don't call Mom to come pick me up. It's probably comical, the little girl in the puffy black jacket and bright-pink rain boots, trudging gloomily home as if bound by chains. After all, I'm shackled by nothing but sorrow and fear. Fear that burns me, tells me that I will never fit in.

The next day, I walk into school. She runs up to me.

"Hey, can I borrow your calculator? I have a math test first period and I forgot mine," she flashes me a grin that guarantees friendship.

I don't even think, just grab my calculator and hand it to her. "Thanks, you're an angel!" she squeals, full of unnatural excitability. I smile, bitterly, my eyes stinging. An imperfect angel.

Words Like Knives

In seventh grade, I look in the mirror and don't see the girl that has always been there. The new girl is different. She is more muscular, but I don't see that. I can't see past the fact that she looks different than a few waif-like girls in my ballet class, and I hate that. I look in the mirror and see fat.

It is an irrational struggle with image, self-inflicted and painful. Every day I look into the mirror and feel dissatisfied with my body and then frustrated with myself for being so shallow.

So on a dark night at a sleepover, I swallow my pride and voice what I have been grappling with. It is so hard to ask my friend the shameful question, but this is a real struggle for me, confusing and graphic and I have to get it off my chest.

"No, Jade," she replies to my whispered self-doubt. "You're beautiful. You are one of the most beautiful people I know, inside and out." I know this should reassure me, but it doesn't.

I work hard in ballet and push myself in cross-country be-cause the painful hard work enables me to put my secret insecurity out of my head. It's a surprise to no one but me when I develop an overuse injury. Suddenly I am limited in a way I have never been before, and I hate it.

One day, sitting on the side of the darkened dance studio, it finally sinks in. Thin doesn't guarantee good technique. Only hard work can do that.

When I recover enough to dance, I look in the mirrors of the ballet studio to correct my technique instead of to compare myself to everyone around me. I realize that muscle keeps me safe in my dancing, and I stop obsessing over my body. But I never stop noticing.

On a balmy summer evening, I nudge my friend. "Do you think I'm fat?" I question her.

"Why would I think that?" she asks bluntly.

"Well, I'm afraid guys won't like me because I have small boobs and big legs," I explain, and lower my gaze, ashamed to admit I'm still hanging on to my fear.

"Look, if all he wants are the breasts and the thighs, tell him to take it on down to KFC," she snickers. I'm surprised to find myself chuckling as well. This might not have been the way I thought this conversation would go, but at the moment it's the best way it could have gone, because the gash in my heart, whittled out after months of self-doubt, is beginning to heal. I'm accepted for who I am, and that makes all the difference.

So it's a shock to hear someone instruct me months later: "Don't eat that, you'll get fat."

The Streets of Jerusalem

MOLLY BREITBART, Grade 12, Age 17. Edgemont High School, Scarsdale, NY, Michael Devito, *Educator*

The streets are cobblestone here. Not like the cobblestones back home, though. These cobblestones have heard stories and felt wars. They've embraced fallen bodies and supported the arches of prophets. Our cobblestones have only seen the undersides of lapdogs or the soles of children's feet walking home from the church nursery school.

I always wonder what sidewalks eat. At home, they subsist mostly on cigarette butts and highway wildflowers, spare change and wads of chewing gum. But here, the sidewalks are healthier. Granted, cigarette butts still decorate their edges, but they have an easy, Terracotta glow from the relentless sunshine.

Here the aroma isn't of lawn mower exhaust and the diner down the hill—it's something out of an Arabian fairy tale. The air sags with saffron and the heady, berry-twinged perfume of hookah pipes. The fruit vendors with their lee-chi rinds and bulbous mangoes contribute the next layer, and at the heart of it, there's the tangy scent of anticipation.

I walked these streets, overwhelmed by color, by accents speaking languages I could never dream of understanding.

This place is mystic even to an agnostic. I believe nothing, and that's allowed here. Reputation aside, I don't have to regard any of the gods that rule over these quarters. I can blend in with the passerby, a nameless face in a throng of merchants and tourists and residents. No one asks any questions, which suits me fine.

I approach the Wall and can tell at once that it knows my secrets, the very worst ones. How I haven't properly spoken to my brother for the six months before this trip, how I don't floss the way I tell the dentist I do, how my "I love you"s are hollow. The Wall also knows every eyelash wish I've ever made, every glimmer of hope I deposit into my future, collecting aspirations as scattered and sparkly as the contents of a snow globe.

The Wall is not a gossip magazine. The Wall is not an adjudicator. The Wall does not judge.

So I kneel before it, run my fingers over its dimples and cracks. I marvel at how people—not machines, not superheroes, not angels—built this so many moons ago. Would I have been able to withstand such a feat had I been born in 19 B.C.E.? The strain on my body and mind would have annihilated me, and I'm ashamed of that. When did we all become so fragile? The answer lies somewhere between the pages of history textbooks, but we are too lazy, or maybe too terrified, to figure it out. We are the rebirth of zombie culture, soldered to our motherboards, constantly deleting our memory cards to make more room for this virtual reality we occupy. Briefly, I envisioned a return to 19 B.C.E. in a flying DeLorean. My presence would contaminate history, would make my brother disappear from family photos. Perhaps some things are better left untouched. I pondered over age and the ageless. The Wall has survived my oldest ancestors, yet it looks the same as it does on my dad's postcards from 1983. It's seen an incomparable array of faces, heard their prayers. Now those people are long dead, their prayers in limbo; the Wall is alive, clutching their memories inside of its pores. Those believers, those years . . . nothing lasts anymore, does it? Not love—divorces scream at us from supermarket check-out lines, infidelity no longer a taboo. Not friendship—we lose touch, slipping from fully waffled fingers to neighboring knuckles to the pads of our pinkies. Certainly not promises. Promises are plastic now, disposable. We try to recycle them in vain. But the Wall is here forever, even though forever is a figment.

Before me now are more masses, segregated by gender for reasons I cannot fathom. Do testosterone and estrogen really distract from earnest prayer? We are all human beings, regardless of our genitalia. We are all Molotov cocktails of vice and virtue, and sometimes we need to believe in something beyond ourselves. If I were to gaze down at the spectacle from atop a hill, I'd be able to see the divide in all of its glory, a zebra stripe of sexism. The scene made me think of all of the orthodox weddings I'd attended in my lifetime. I remembered how I was never allowed to dance with my father, how I seemed to be missing out on some boisterous comedy on the male side of the ballroom. I sympathized with the women at the Wall, heads cloaked in white, isolated from the davening men, whose hats covered heads stuffed with archaic concepts of equality.

Folded to the size of my thumb nail was a letter that I wrote in our hotel room (I was too terrified of the wandering eyes of my fellow passengers to attempt writing it on the plane). My writing was small enough for the ants to read, a confession printed painstakingly, early in the morning when I was warped by jet lag and plagued by the past. It hurt to write it, but now I felt lighter.

I will never tell you what it said. Mostly because I don't remember the exact words. But I do remember the emotions I left tucked into the crevices of the Wall: the fear and the hatred I abandoned, the guilt I left to die. Laughter accumulated within me and I felt it rise like the bubbles in champagne, filling the space between my shoulder blades and telling me that I too could fly.

Once more I walked through Jerusalem, a free spirit.

Contagion

KAIN KIM, Grade 11, Age 16. Bergen County Academies, Hackensack, NJ. David Wilson, *Educator*

When I am seven and Ah-Rim is six, a new boy transfers to our homeroom.

Half of his face is ravaged with tiny red dots, pricks of inflamed skin roughly textured like braille, and when he enters through the sliding door, the entire class breaks out in excited whispers. Half of me wants to avoid his embarrassed gaze, turn around and pretend like he doesn't exist, but the other half of me can't stop staring at his horribly mutilated complexion. It looks as if he's dunked the right side of his head into the hot oil they fry my potatoes in at the local cookery.

(Contagion: 1. The communication of disease by direct or indirect contact; 2. Harmful or undesirable contact or influence.)

Our teacher curtly introduces him as Min-Jeong, that he'll be staying with us as a fellow classmate this semester, and that she expects us all to treat him with courtesy and respect. This goes without saying, of course. By the time Min-Jeong has settled into his seat, looking as stiff as a corpse, it's gotten around the entire room that his new name is Disease Boy. Ah-Rim elbows me in the ribs and snickers at the nickname. My desk mate leans across the table and hisses at me, "We'll greet him properly at the statue after school. Pass it on."

His eyes flicker with mischief, and he grins expectantly at me. I laugh and pass it on.

(It's always struck me as funny how adults assume you can't remember anything from before you were five or six years old, when rather, the memories are like a series of frames from a film in my head, crystal in clarity and glaring with color and life. That's not a memory, they'll say laughing, and pat your head condescendingly. You probably saw a photograph, and you're mistaking it for something else that happened much, much later. I wonder if the more we grow, the less we remember, like those memories are captured in sheets of negative that will just keep piling on top of one another over the years, until the original picture is so disfigured and blackened by what came after that you can't even remember what it was of in the first place.)

It's an unusually cold day for May. Min-Jeong stands by the statue, a stone memorial of the school's founder, and waits, book bag clutched defensively to his thin chest. This Disease Boy isn't stupid. He's seen the looks and heard the hissed insults, felt the quick, lithe feet shooting out from underneath desks to trip his own large, clumsy ones and felt the unanimous, hushed response it drew from the class. His eyes are like the sleek, flat stones that my dad and I use to skip across the surface of the park lake. They are hard and glassy and reflect the gray sky in chiseled chunks.

"What is he, stupid?" Ah-Rim mutters to me. "Why isn't he running?"

Already a small throng of kids has gathered around the statue. Nothing too important is happening yet, just some minor taunting and name-calling. Min-Jeong is holding his own. A few adults walk by on the commute home from work and glare at us in disdain. We pull faces and sneer at them, too.

My desk mate, the one who had gathered us here today, steps forward first when a nice little crowd has formed. You can tell he's glad to have an audience. He slowly picks up a rock, a solid piece of gravel about the size of my fist. He tosses it in the air and catches it. Toss, catch. Toss, catch. We all watch the rock as if hypnotized, following its path with our eyes as it arcs neatly through the air and lands with a smack in the boy's palm. No one is taunting Disease Boy now—ominous silence echoes throughout the grounds, more deafening than the raucous chatter from before. Min-Jeong is staring stoically at the ground.

Without any warning, the rock suddenly sails through the air and hits Min-Jeong on the shoulder.

It's like the world was on mute, and a switch has just been flipped. The sound rushes back at full force again, boys screeching in wild abandon, girls screaming and giggling in excitement. Everyone hunts for rocks on the ground to throw. Pebbles and stones and chunks of gravel hurtle through space and deflect off of Disease Boy, who's not responding at all. He just stands there, an island of resigned peace and serenity amongst the cacophony. The statue behind him smiles down benevolently on the scene.

"Help me look for rocks," Ah-Rim is saying. The tips of her straight black braids nearly brush the ground in her concentration as she bends over the lot. "Everybody's taking the good ones."

What happens next, I don't quite remember too well. I think I ran away, or pretended to help Ah-Rim look for a while. I did not help the boy with the spots on his face.

Throwing rocks at him with the rest of my classmates would have been less cowardly.

(I will realize, later, much to my unrestrained horror, that he lives in my apartment building. We will wait together in interminable silence for the elevator to reach the lobby. The first thing he will say to me, quietly and without making eye contact, will be, "It's not contagious." My response will be, "I never asked." Then, in the elevator, feeling as if I've got to say something, as if I have to redeem myself to this boy who I watched get pelted with stones before my very eyes: "Why didn't you just run away? You waited for them. Like an idiot." He will not say anything, simply step out onto his floor without any words of farewell. And I will realize, much, much later, that the silence was all the answer I needed. That what he protected out there, facing down all of class 2-AB in the enduring, tolerant silence of a god, was something more significant than maintaining any physical manifestation.)

Slowly but surely, we become friends. It's a unique, twisted relationship, to say the least. I do all the talking; he listens. If it wasn't for the answers he'd give to our teacher in class, I'd be sure he was either deaf or mute. Sometimes, not often, I'd get the impression that I am conversing with a brick wall, and would scream at him to say something, anything, so I didn't feel like I was talking to myself; but then he'd simply look at me, and smile, and that would be enough for me to apologize and fall into a shameful silence.

Ah-Rim and I don't hang out anymore. On the rare occasions that we make eye contact with one another, she will glare at me and quickly turn to whisper something to the beady-eyed girls who have started to follow her more and more lately, like faithful pets trailing after their owner. Even these brief encounters eventually peter to a complete stop, and after a while I can't even imagine that this giggling, pigtailed girl held a role in my life at one time.

This is precisely why I'm so dubious when she rings my door one morning and asks me to go rollerblading with her.

"There's something I want to do."

"Okay."

Our apartment complex is built on top of a hill, so that the buildings slowly slope up on a gradual incline toward the sun. This means that there's only one way to leave the complex— down the main road, which is dangerously steep and flattens into the heavy rush of perpetual traffic. Parents go to great pains to keep the scooter- and rollerblading-loving children of the neighborhood away from the main road. Once you gather enough momentum and speed, which won't take long because of the steep nature of the hill, it's nearly impossible to turn at the last second into the nearby alleyway to avoid the cars. We've had accidents before—none fatal, thankfully, but enough to establish the hill as a permanent hazard zone.

"We're going to skate down the hill," Ah-Rim declares, eyes shining. "It's easy. Just watch me."

She does it, sailing effortlessly down in her skates and making a slow, wide turn into the alleyway, a dark, vacuous pit that lacerates one of the tall brick walls that line the base of the hill. After a while, she emerges from the alley, skates in one hand, and starts making the long trek up the pavement in her bare feet, face turned up toward the sun expectantly. She motions for me to skate down too.

I don't move.

She reaches the pinnacle of the hill, standing next to me once again, flushed and bright-eyed.

"Well?" She gestures impatiently toward the road. "Are you going to do it or not?"

There's a string coiled between us, taut with tension and worn thin. She's testing its durability, gently tugging and yanking, but it refuses to snap. It's up to me to break it off completely, I realize.

(Vicariousness: Act of performing, exercising, or suffering in place of another.)

"Sure." I fasten my helmet. "No big deal."

Skating down the hill is the equivalent to flying. I feel weightless, buoyant in the whip of the rushing air current, arms spread about as if I'm going to take flight. The alley draws up beside me all too quickly, its gap-toothed entrance a gaping mouth waiting to swallow me. I angle my feet and turn into it, exhilaration and satisfaction plunging through my veins. What I wasn't expecting, however, is the concrete wall waiting too closely on the other end of the alley.

(What my mother says to me, later, becomes nothing more than a harsh, discordant noise buzzing in my ears, a recorder skipping brokenly to emit the same despairing sounds. *Ai-goo, how could you have been so stupid? How many times have I told you not to go down there?*

When I had struggled back up to the top of the hill, half of my face mangled and bleeding, Ah-Rim had vanished. It stings more than the burn of the salve my mother applies with her birdlike fingers, her delicate touches light and airy.)

We wait for the elevator together, watching as the numbers slowly light up, one by one, cheerfully chiming its way down. He thoughtfully contemplates the ragged scars that cover the entire left side of my face. The doctor says they will remain there for quite a while before they fade entirely.

"I didn't run away," I say.

He says nothing, as usual, but his understanding gaze says enough. *It's not the same thing.* I shrug and grin at him, an expression of undebilitating joy and recklessness that only a seven-year-old could wear.

The Great Grandfather of My Myths

EMILY GREEN, Grade 12, Age 17. Appomattox Regional Governor's School, Petersburg, VA, Cindy Cunningham, *Educator*

My great grandfather used to grow bonsai trees until his hands couldn't shape them anymore, until he couldn't fit his gnarled fingers into tiny metal scissors. He tilled his garden, willed stubborn plants to grow from sand until he couldn't walk. My mother called him Jiji, but I called him Ookii jiji, big grandfather. He came from the same beach town I had been born in, but I always imagined him from the mountains, his birth miraculous; he was the boy born of thunder, of ancient and mystic mountains, of Japan itself.

His gait was confident, his shoulders broader than the average Japanese. People bowed to him in the street as he passed, seeing his sharp face and knowing that he was of a different time; a time when the men of Japan worked with their hands and backs, and wives stayed home to care for the children. My great grandfather never learned how to work a stove, that was women's work.

But he was gentle. I would sit cross-legged on the tatami of his living room while he reclined on a floor pillow and he spoke to me in Japanese, his voice deep and hearty, gruff from old age. He would ask me questions and know that I understood him, even though I was the American child. *Kyo nani suru no, Emi? Kyo nani shitai?* He used to speak my name like it was an inside joke between the two of us, a chuckle in his voice. My great grandfather was tall. But even though I couldn't watch it happen, time was curling his spine, robbing him of his height day by day. Gravity and age were compressing him into someone who could only be mortal.

Every three years meant my visit to Japan, and the whirlwind of "You've gotten so big, you've gotten so pretty, you've grown so old, Emi." But I returned each year, always shocked by how many more wrinkles my uncle had, how much more tired my aunt looked, or which beloved family dog had died. Unbeknownst to my Japanese relatives, time did not stop for them. America was not some place where their little Emi, the doll-child, would go for years and gain more height, more strength, more maturity only to come back home to them. The mirror didn't show the changes, but photos did, my memories did, my eyes did. They grew old.

My great grandfather had to put away his bonsais. He stopped asking me questions. He stopped walking.

My grandfather and his brothers, my great-uncles, had to put him in a nursing home eventually, visiting as often as they could, feeding him canned clementines with a plastic spoon. One day, they apologized for bringing him canned grapefruit, and I wondered if it mattered at all, if he could know the difference. I wondered if he cared that his sons were gathered around him feeding him like an infant; one of them divorced twice, one of them about to retire from work at the recycling plant, one of them trying his best to keep his father's plot of land alive. I wondered if he remembered the one missing from the circle, the son who had died decades ago from kidney failure.

The oldest asked if the old man wanted to drink the fruit juice left at the bottom of the can, and he nodded his head lazily. Alright, the son said, get ready now, and tilted the can to his father's lips. Suddenly, he coughed, loudly and painfully. The sound startled me, and I looked from the window to my great grandfather's hunched frame, quaking with a noise so loud I thought it could shatter him. The son was apologizing, and everyone was laughing. He spoke in chortling Japanese, "We're sorry," he said, "I poured that too fast, didn't I?" He threw the can away, saying that that was probably enough for today. "Hey, hey! Stop trying to kill the old man," the youngest son snickered. I could see that my mother's initial concern had faded with their humor, but I was still on edge, sitting on the windowsill and trying not to cry.

My grandmother had told me that talking would be good for him. She had always been my great grandfather's favorite daughter-in-law, that was no secret. My grandparents' marriage had been arranged because my great grandfather had liked this girl who came from a tea farm in Haruno-cho. She filled her role well, and in her cheeriest, most interested voice, she attempted to engage him. "He can tell time still," she said, "he can still read his watch. Ask him what time it is."

His eyes dropped to his thin wrists, and someone pulled back his sleeve. He replied in gasps, like a drowning man, like air was precious. "You must stretch your legs, Jiji. You must move them every day, do you understand? Bend them like this." And my grandmother worked his knees, massaged his joints. "Look, he can still make a fist. Jiji, show them. Make a fist like this." She pushed my grandfather to say something, and he protested that he simply had nothing to say. I was still on my window perch, watching my own hand forge a fist and uncurl itself again and again, terrified that I'd be chosen to initiate something.

His legs were frozen into bending, his arms permanently limp by his sides. His skin speckled and stretched like the dried fish we'd buy in the markets. His hands were cold, his fingers skinny and worn. Time had taken his hands, and his legs, but I still prayed that it wouldn't take all of his mind.

Then my grandmother began to play a game that I assumed happened every time they visited him here in this room too small to hold our entire family. "What is her name? What is my name? Who is he?" I watched them go around the room and laugh when he could not name his youngest son, instead only commenting that he had gotten fatter. They made it around the circle to my mother, and I could see from my seat on the windowsill that she was trying to keep her smile. "And who is this, Jiji?" My mother beamed, encouraged him, "Yes, yes, Jiji, who am I?" He stared at her for what seemed like an endless time, lengthened further by silence. "Ma," he said. "Yes, yes, Jiji, Ma . . .?" and eventually my grandmother gave in. "That's Mayumi, isn't it, Jiji? Ma-Yu-Mi." My mother smiled in a way that one would smile to a toddler; she nodded heartily, confirming that yes, she was Mayumi.

I knew that eventually it would come to me. My grandmother pointed to my face, and his gazed followed slowly. "Who is that, Jiji?"

Once, when I was younger, my great grandfather had called me a "mixed blood," a derogatory term for children who are born out of the blood of a gaijin, a foreigner. My mother was shocked, but said nothing, knowing that he meant nothing by it, because in his time they had no other word. And after I was born I became Emiri, his great granddaughter, Mayumi's girl. A few days out of every two or three years is all he saw of me, and yet I want to believe he loved me fiercely in the small windows of my visits. He saw me in the year my mother cut my hair into horrible bangs and said they were cute. He looked in awe and curiosity when I showed him the odd bits of metal I had gotten to straighten my teeth. He nodded at my plans to go to Nagoya and buy colors and bleaches for my hair, and I looked in and saw as time seemed to take him in leaps and lurches.

The bonsais were no longer on shelves outside of his home. He could no longer grow his watermelon by himself. He couldn't bike to his garden plot. He could not speak. He could not stand. He could not remember.

My great grandfather looked at me and I tried to smile encouragingly, as if my smile could give him my name. I'd like to think that in that moment, thoughts swirled in his mind, that something was still there. That all the coins he had given me to buy candy at the grocery store, the grape gelatin cups I'd always ask for, that salted watermelon slices, that seashells and sand and my clumsy steps as a toddler were swirling in his mind. I was ashamed I couldn't hold his gaze, feeling guilt for something neither he nor I could control, feeling like time and distance was something I could have stopped, changed. I was not the grandchild there every day to ask him what time it was, spoon his favorite fruit into the mouth that opened mechanically until it had had enough.

His eyes kept steady, they had never changed. His jaw worked as if it was trying to recall how to behave, how to form words.

"You've . . . you've gotten so big, haven't you?"

The last time I saw him, I had come to say goodbye because I was leaving for America in three days. I asked if I could take his picture, and he stared into the camera as my mother and I tried not to cry in front of him, because that seemed too hopeless. My mother assured him that we would be back, that we would come again in a few years to visit, but then in his eyes I saw something that we both understood. Something I would not say, and something he could not articulate with the throat that made him sound an animal.

My great grandfather had always been a wise man, a fairy-tale giant, something mystical and ancient. He knew as well as I did that he would not be waiting for us in a wheelchair, in that nursing home plastered in the child-like artwork of its doddering, senile patients, but in the house he had built with his own hands, before they gnarled themselves like the pines our beach town is known for. That I could find him again only in a black-and-white picture framed above the family altar, the air conditioner billowing incense smoke around that tiny living room. In my mind, he belonged to neither, was not someone who could be confined, by body, by any frame, any room, but time has a way of making choices.

I returned to America, and we did not hear about his death until after the funeral.

My grandmother knew that we couldn't scrounge up the money for four expensive plane tickets in a matter of days, didn't want us to feel guilty. She didn't want me to think I could have changed anything, a young girl's hands can't hold back those of a clock, couldn't, and she didn't ask me to try. But I couldn't help it, I tried, and I still saw it, everything. My grandfather and his brothers with long, thin, black, lacquered pine chopsticks picking the bone out of fine ashes. I saw it, someone carving another name onto our family grave. I saw a sea of white and black, heads held down, weighed by either politeness or the loss of a father, a good man, a relic of an older Japan. Stone statues of Shinto gods and Buddhas with their arms outstretched watching with half-open eyes, and no promises about fate. I could smell the incense the monks burn, and I knew that if I squinted, the gray sand and the gray sky would lose its horizon.

I know I will return to the maze of stone pillars I always visit when I come to Japan, to the graveyard that I've known since before I could understand why I prayed before it. My grandmother will give me flowers to hold, and we'll put them on the graves of generations of family I never knew; a great-uncle's first wife who passed young from cancer, the son who had died of kidney failure because the doctors of his time didn't know how to help. I can't help but think about my great grand-father's ashes sitting against the granite of his tombstone, how the stone obelisk will be about his height, back when we used to sit in his air-conditioned living room, me eating grape gela-tin, and him asking what I planned to do with today.

The Feminist in Me

TUHFA BEGUM, Grade 12, Age 17. Vanguard High School, New York, NY, Josleen Wilson, *Educator*

It started with an insult, when we collided at the front door of school at 8 o'clock on a Monday morning. I dropped my armful of this week's feminist posters, and they scattered across the threshold and back down the front steps.

He didn't help but stood watching me as I struggled to pick them up and tuck them under my arm.

"What's the matter with you anyway?" he asked. He had that slouchy, dumb look on his face that some boys covet.

"Excuse me?"

"Why don't you take cooking class like the other girls do? You'd learn something useful, instead of putting up those stupid posters every week."

This was not a line from an '80s sitcom. Before I could give my classmate a stern lecture about the relevance of the feminist movement, we were saved by the bell and on our way to the next class.

I've been a feminist since long before I knew what the word meant. I was born in Bangladesh, unaware that I was the first female in my family to be delivered in a hospital, the first to receive a birth certificate, the first to be recognized and seen as having potential. My grandfather defied the traditional gender roles of Bengali society, ignoring the admonishments of local imams and performing a Muslim prayer ceremony for me in the hospital. The ceremony was typically conducted to celebrate the birth of the first-born male in a family. Even after my birth, he consistently defied gender norms by teaching me to read and write in English, and by making sure that I sat amongst the men in the mosque, rather than being herded off to a dark corner like the other women and children. He wanted my voice to be heard.

My mother never received the benefit of his feminist support. When she was born, my grandfather was young, poor, and living in a backwards village. He arranged a marriage for her to my father when she was twenty years old, hoping that one day her husband would take her to America, the land of promise. My mother had no choice. Even today in Bangladesh, and in many other countries around the world, the expectation for a girl is to have no expectations.

I immigrated to the United States with my parents when I was three years old. My awareness of feminism and gender inequality quickly broadened. While other little girls in school were ardent followers of the Disney princesses, I imagined a princess who could save herself and her kingdom, without the aid of a prince or a knight in shining armor. I was a devoted fan of Lisa Simpson, who was constantly belittled by the other characters in *The Simpsons*. I admired her smart mouth and her feminist beliefs. I recognized myself in Susan Pevensie who was cast out of the mythical Narnia because she refused to conform and insisted on growing up. I sympathized with the Susan in Neil Gaiman's short story "The Problem of Susan," in which Susan Pevensie spent the rest of her life rebelling against conformity and challenging societal expectations.

Throughout my childhood, I practically lived in the local library, breathing in books and stories. My mother always reminded me to not take for granted the limitless opportunities available to me in the United States. While the mothers of many of my classmates were doctors or lawyers, my mother worked at a minimum-wage job, serving fast food while juggling taking care of her family. Her selfless dedication to doing what is best for her family has always inspired me to work hard and persevere against obstacles.

Relatives and family friends frequently belittled me for my feminist beliefs. My first homework assignment in middle school history class was to create a board game using historical events that we had learned in elementary school.

My board game had many categories, including the Revolutionary War, Manifest Destiny, and the Civil War. I remember sitting on the floor of the room I shared with my brother and creating a new category I called "The Suffrage Movement and Feminism." A family friend walked into my room to chat with my brother and me. He studied the new category that I had added to my board game.

After serious "contemplation," he said, "Aren't you going to add something about men's rights? It's we men that have to carry the burden of feminine nonsense." I was too young to stand up to him, but through many experiences like this, I learned that criticism comes in many forms, and that bigotry and misogyny are alive and well—and loud.

In high school, I took extra courses at colleges in New York, and volunteered at the Housing Works Bookstore (a nonprofit bookstore helping people with AIDS). Last summer, I interned at the Bella Abzug Leadership Institute, founded by the daughter of "Battling Bella" herself, and I worked with other young women to bring awareness of the issues of women's rights and all human rights to the public. I learned that women's rights ARE human rights.

This was the turning point where I turned lifelong belief into activism. I began making my posters about happenings in the news about the global abuse of women. I staged little events in the hallways and handed out flyers.

Through all of my efforts and struggles, my mother always stood by me, from the warm glasses of milk she would hand to me during late-night study sessions, to the Girls Write Now annual public readings, where she clapped the loudest when I read my work. Even so, her long work hours and my demanding academic schedule meant that we spent little time together.

One day, after having two wisdom teeth removed, I moaned and sulked around the house, until finally, I followed my mother into uncharted territory—the kitchen. I've never helped out in the kitchen. I feared that stepping inside once would lead to me never stepping out. My deepest fear was that one day I would be confined to the oppressive standards of my female ancestors.

They were expected to marry young, cook, clean, and bear sons. They were also expected to do most of these relentless chores in the kitchen. To me, this seemed like a miserable and lonely existence. It certainly clashed with my idea of feminism.

But as I stood in the doorway, watching my mother—she was wearing her faded blue jeans and salwar kameez while she prepared dinner—I saw that she didn't look miserable at all. She was gossiping on the phone in one hand while chopping onions with the other (I still don't know how she does this). She looked happy. I had never wondered if my mother was happy or not. Like the rest of my family, I took for granted that she was always there, providing everything we needed.

My mother said goodbye to her friend and hung up the

phone. Her black hair caught the incandescent lights, and streaks of gray glimmered as she hurriedly pushed her hair off her face and continued working. She started humming along to the Beatles on the radio, and I could not help but remember something that my writing mentor had once told me: "Even in spaces of confinement, women can find liberation."

I lingered in the doorway until she noticed me.

"It's just dal," she said. She stirred the lentils that were soaking in a pot of water. "Come help me clean the next bag of lentils. Look closely to make sure that there are no tiny stones in them."

First step. Second step. On the third step, a loose tile creaked. I found myself inside the kitchen, standing close to my mother's busy hands. We sang along with "Lucy in the Sky With Diamonds" as we worked. I grabbed the other bag of lentils.

My idea of feminism has broadened once again. Perhaps my princess could save herself, save her kingdom, and learn to cook as well.

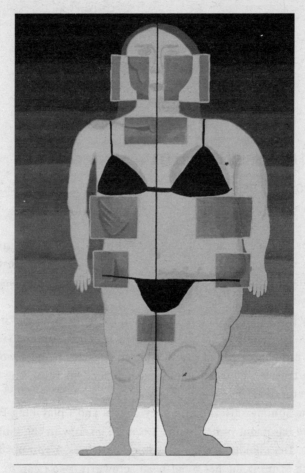

MAIRIN KING, *Inside Out Body Image*, Grade 11, Age 17.
Mystic Valley Regional Charter School, Malden, MA.
Martin Boyle, *Educator*. 2014 Silver Medal

Mimi's Museum

NICHOLAS ELDER, Grade 12, Age 17. Mississippi School for Math and Science, Columbus, MS, Emma Richardson, *Educator*

Bones and fossils line the haphazard metal tool closet in the garage. Mummies sit spine to spine in the oak armoire that stands in the corner of the living room, watching years pass as every new layer of dust settles.

My grandmother is a native Texan living in Wadsworth, Illinois. Her name is Katherine, but she is called Mimi or Yiayia by a growing horde of grandchildren. Besides being a world-class traveler, gourmet chef, and independent tutor, she is a collector of artifacts—tangible history.

One summer afternoon, as my cousin and I play Ping-Pong in the basement of her house, I realize a screw in the table is loose, the obvious source of my missed shots. I run upstairs to ask Mimi if she has a flat-head screwdriver so I can fix the Ping-Pong table and take back my rightful place as grandmaster of the paddle in the family. She leaves the peach half-sliced on the cutting board and heads out to the garage. I, however, am distracted by the nine-month-old cousin attempting to eat Cheerios off the yellow tray of his high chair. Mimi comes back with a rust-tinged screwdriver with a wooden handle. It feels old. Always a nosy kid, I ask her where she got it. She just smiles.

She takes me out to the garage, glancing over the white Lexus and black Buick, but focusing on the beige metal tool shed in the corner. She opens the doors wide, her smile even wider, inviting me to come do more than look. Slight confession: the "bones," "fossils," and "mummies" are actually tools and books, but they hold just as many stories when in the hands of Mimi.

I hold the tools as I would a newborn baby, wary of their strength—amazed at their age. She instead grabs them, thrusting them upon me, confident in their power. She doesn't need any encouragement. She leaps into stories. Her eyes glaze over as years past come flooding back. A few tears spill over the corner of her eyes too. She picks up a wrench, large and dusky gray. It shouts MADE IN THE USA. She remembers her father using it to fix his Model A truck, leaning for hours over the engine of his first car that he babied for thirty-seven years after. The spade that sits in the corner was the one he used to show her how to grow tomatoes, as she still does. Fresh soil from the small bed outside clings to the tip—old tools for old lessons. She hands me a hammer. The head is dented, but the handle is worn smooth. Her father used it to build her a bassinet the week before she was born. That was seventy years ago, but the bassinet still lives, its smooth walnut waves gracing the room I sleep in when I visit.

We head back inside to the living room. The glass-faced armoire looms large. Usually I don't dare go closer than three feet, but as Mimi turns the key—the one with the tassel that always sits in the lock on the glass doors—I can't help but to be sucked in. I shuffle closer and smell undeniable age. Not old-people age, but yellowed-pages, cracked-leather, and dusty-memories age. On the front shelf is a book, no larger than a regular-sized picture, bound in brown worn leather, "Autographs" printed in gold leaf. The only thing she says is that it was her grandfather's, uncle's, and father's before it came to her. Books can tell their own stories.

I am scared to breathe as she sets the book in my hands, worried that the mere stirring of air will crumble the dog-eared tea-colored pages. Names spill out: Lindberg, Dempsey, Temple, Chaplin, and Hepburn. I move on to a set of encyclopedias. I pick out J-K, and recognize Mimi's scrawl in the margins near Jamestown, juggernaut, and kangaroo. It's the same tall, tight writing that has adorned many a Christmas and birthday card. I move on to a cup of nib-tipped pens with wooden paintbrush shafts. They are the kind that you have to dip into an inkwell. I imagine how messy it must have been to write essays—and shudder.

Four generations of stories and artifacts pass through my hands in a mere twenty minutes. I am left in a daze. I eventually resume my Ping-Pong match with my cousin (I lose of course) before helping make dinner, clearing the table, and trudging off to my lonely blow-up mattress. Before I fall asleep, I wonder what things of mine will be passed down to my great-grandchildren, and what stories will accompany them. What things of mine will inspire, will link my world with theirs, a bond across time, a greeting from the grave. I get as far as my name before I pass out in a tangled mess of flowered sheets exposing bare feet and a faint smile.

The Last Summer Leaf

SPENCER GRAYSON, Grade 8, Age 13. Lakeside Middle School, Seattle, WA, Susie Mortensen, *Educator*

Big, Tall, Knows All

Adults are supposed to be smarter than us. After all, they've lived here longer. And they've been to lots of schools and lived in lots of places. They remember to cover their leftovers with plastic before they put them in the fridge. They are allowed to use computers for longer than half an hour. They never cry, and they never ever make mistakes.

But adults don't play, and I don't think that's a very smart idea. Playing is what gets you through the hard stuff, like being nervous for the class play or not seeing your friend anymore because she's at a different school. Playing is like entering a different world, a world where girls wear long satin dresses but can still climb trees, where animals actually talk back to you, and you can forget everything that's bad for a little while.

My daddy should play more. Sometimes he sits at his computer late at night, brows furrowed like a caterpillar. Mommy says he's worried about work and not to bother him. I don't, but I think if he took more time to enjoy himself he would never put his head in his hands. Wouldn't you rather go on an adventure, with pirates and horses and princesses, instead of sitting alone in the basement, scratchy brown rug, and computer screen with a blank page?

But who would listen to me? Not grown-ups. I can hear their big voices, confident and strong, echoing in my head like a brass drum. That's very nice, Maggie. You remember that for when you're older.

A Gray Dress

My family is quiet during the long drive to Portland. My father's face is expressionless, but his eyes are sad as he grips the steering wheel with his knuckles white, looking straight ahead. My mother is silent too. She is pretty in her black dress, but it is a sad color on her. Black, I think, is the saddest color, because it is the color people wear to funerals.

My sister is only six, and that's too young to know what's going on around you, but I am older than her and I know why we have taken this long, stifling drive all the way from home in Seattle to here, where my daddy grew up and where my cousins live. Because Pops, my Pops and my daddy's dad, is no longer hooked up to the clear tubes and whirring machines in the hospital. He will never smile proudly when Natalie and I talk about our school projects, and when we drive down for Thanksgiving, we will not visit him in the home. We will take the exit and drive onto the freeway, while he rests underneath a white plaque with his name, covered with pretty blue and purple flowers.

When we reach the place they're going to have his funeral, my mother hands Natalie and me each a wad of clothing. "Put on your dresses, girls," she says in a strong but slightly quivering voice. We quickly obey, slipping out of our shorts and shirts and pulling on white knee-high socks and flats. We then tug on our dresses. The skirt reaches my knees, pleated and un-wrinkled. The sleeves are long, encompassing my skinny arms, and there is a little tie of cloth that holds the neck together. My dress is gray. Gray all over, from the pleats of the skirt to the neckline. Gray is an okay color, and I do feel pretty in this dress. My sister is wearing the same dress as me, but in a dark periwinkle. Her color looks like a streak of the sunset, while I . . . I don't know.

Other people are walking into the funeral home as well. We follow the crowd and take our seats next to my grandmother, Nanny, and my cousins and aunt and uncle. They hug us, say hello, but without their usual cheerfulness. The adults all resemble my parents; the smiles stolen from their faces, but my cousins just look confused.

The rabbi walks up to the microphone beyond the pews and begins to speak. He welcomes everyone, and then he starts to talk about Pops. He says some very nice things, about what a great personality Pops was, how much his children and grand-children loved him. I sneak a glance over at my father. There are tears, tears like diamonds slowing sliding down his cheeks. I have never seen Daddy cry before. I have never seen an adult cry before. I turn my head and my mother is crying too, Mom-my who is always strong. Every adult in this room is crying or blotting their eyes with Kleenex. I do not cry.

I do not cry.

After the service, Nanny tells Natalie and me how nice we look in our dresses. We both say thank you, but my words feel hollow to me. I pull at this gray dress, this gray dress that should be pretty. I turn around and I whisper goodbye to Pops, ashamed of my sad gray dress. I should have worn something the color of jade, like Pops's favorite ring he used to wear. Or blue, my favorite color and the color of the sky, a beautiful and free color, like how Pops is right now, free from the machines and tangles of tubes that barely kept him alive. Not gray. Pops would want people to be happy at his funeral, happy that he had lived a good life. Not gray.

Good Things

On the coldest of evenings, when the rain pounds on the tired glass with an iron fist, my mother lights the pumpkin candle. It is the dark, rusty auburn of fallen leaves, its scent gentle yet intoxicating, sweeter than sugar dusting a croissant, cleansing as a freshly bought bar of soap.

When the fire is flickering but cannot keep out the chill, the smell of the pumpkin candle wafting from the kitchen warms from the inside out. Like a fuzzy blanket, its smell drapes over you, reminds you that the cold will not stay forever. Good things are coming, it says, good things. With a crack of the lighter, I remember the chatter of family coming to stay. Puffy bread straight out of the oven, drenched in gooey golden gravy. Smiles. The laughter of my cousins, clear and real, forgotten during those freezing months. Even when you come tromping through the front door, assignments and quizzes crowding every corner of your brain like dusty boxes in the attic and worry creasing your face, the cozy scent of pumpkin is enough to calm your thoughts and take you somewhere else. Someplace where life is gentler and being stressed is a scarce emotion. Someplace where loved ones beckon you with open arms, where sun and smiles will come again, and where the air smells of pumpkin candles.

Memoir of Imagination

KELLEY SCHLISE, Grade 7, Age 12. St. Robert Elementary School, Shorewood, WI. Marisa Riepenhoff, *Educator*

Imagination fades as you grow up. But pieces float back to you sometimes, and you can relish again the sweet taste of pretending. When I was younger, maybe in second or third grade, and still in my phase of obsession with horses, I would go outside in the brittle piercing autumn air. I would wear what I thought were my stable clothes. I would scooter back and forth on Concordia, the street alongside my corner house, but I would never bring my scooter around the sharp corners that ended my domain. I would stay on one side of the street too. My scooter wasn't just a scooter to me, though. It was my horse.

My horse, with two red handlebars extending off the top of the dull silver metal pole that was its body. My horse with two red wheels, one in front and the other in the back. I jumped over lines of chalk I drew in the uneven cement of my block. They became vertical jumps, oxers, combinations, and more varied jumps that I distinguished on the pavement with designs and words. I jumped and jumped for long periods of time outside, lifting my front wheel over all the jumps. I always stood on the scooter with my left foot and pushed my right deep into the pavement, into the sidewalk, remembering to always wear shoes when scootering so the brake on my scooter wouldn't burn my foot. This was my imagination game.

My familiar red Razor scooter stood tall at its maximum height, raised proudly all the way to the top. The ripped red handle bar on the right side was covered by a shiny bright-blue piece of duct tape, a special trademark of my scooter. And on that scooter, I knew the sidewalk like my best friend. I knew where all the cracks were, which parts were smooth and rough, which blocks were longer and shorter, which parts of my friend I had to be careful traveling over. I knew where little sprouts of green dug through the solid cement, yearning for the sun. The stretch of sidewalk was my sidewalk, my arena.

When I scootered, I let my mind do gymnastics as I imagined stories and characters who rode horses. I would make a protagonist, a kind girl who was the best rider at the stable that blossomed in my mind. Then a mean girl would take shape as the antagonist, someone who was snobby and rich but also talented at riding. This person often had two friends to flank her. I would devise the stable in its glory, the layout of the stalls, the tack room with each character's gleaming saddles and bridles, and the instructor and owner. I would also picture the clothes of each character, and of course their horses. I would take breaks from my scooter races at the corners of the block or just simply sit on the sloping step up to the yard and ponder my characters' personalities.

I remember shiny black-haired Ruby and her friends: Brianna, who had extremely white-blond hair that she sometimes wore in a french braid, and Serena, who had blond hair with brown highlights. These were the mean girls, all pretty and excellent riders. Ruby's horse was black and Serena had a horse named Rose. Then there was the instructor's favorite rider, Cecelia. She was a pretty blond, and the best one at the stable. Cecelia would always be in a good mood, and she had a perfect horse.

I remember shooting down the block, so fast I never wanted

to stop. The wind pressing against my rosy cheeks, my fingers numb. My blue stopwatch would hang around my neck, bouncing against my chest as I lifted the front wheel of my scooter off the ground over the chalk lines. Once my course ended, at the corner, I would skid to a stop and quickly jam my finger onto the stop button. I would ride the course multiple times, pretending to be a different character each time. I would record times for each character and see who had the best time, competing against myself in different points of view.

I remember, too, riding scooters with my friend Delilah. She was a year older, but we were best friends, and she liked horses too. She would bring her newer red Razor scooter over to play, and the two of us would go out in the cold and crisp air in our jeans and plaid shirts, daydreaming about horses and real riding.

We made dressage tests and used trees and street signs as markers, writing down tests and making efforts to memorize them. We critiqued each other and devised ways to do each gait, from free walk to collected canter. We posted and sat to the trot, awkwardly moving in a back-and-forth motion as we moved, and we scootered long strokes for the canter, one with our scooters.

Riding my scooter horse was a way for me to let my imagination run in all different directions, in territory that I enjoyed. It also let me "ride horses," something I was afraid to actually do. Being out in the fresh air, pushing my foot along the cement, was a carefree time for me to play, and it still remains a fond memory for me. Today, I don't scooter anymore. I sometimes sit quietly and imagine my dream bedroom, or I mentally select clothes for an occasion. But it never satisfies as much as being outside on the sidewalk, racing with the wind, faster than all the cold air that rushed by, worriless and fearless.

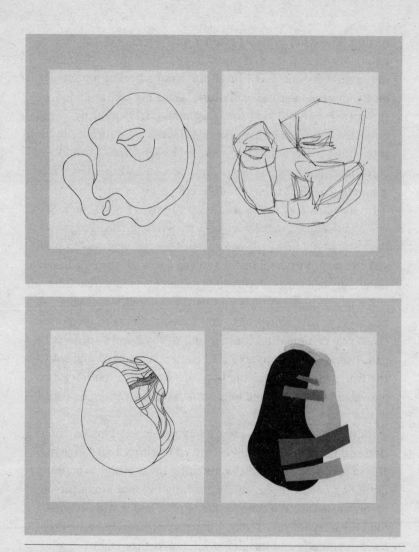

YIHAN CHOU, *Android No. 2*, *A Relativistic Model of the Universe*, *Android No. 3*, *Before the Waveform Collapses*, Grade 12, Age 17, East Brunswick High School, East Brunswick, NJ. Sharron Liu, *Educator*. 2014 Silver Medal with Distinction Art Portfolio

Long-Awaited Aid Finally Reaches Flood-Ravaged Philippines

CHRISTOPHER ZHENG, Grade 11, Age 16. Cherry Creek High School, Greenwood Village, CO, Kathy McInerney, *Educator*

Facebook "likes" arrive at the most devastated areas after Super Typhoon Haiyan

NEWS IN BRIEF • World News • Natural Disasters • Global • ISSUE 49/42 • Nov 18, 2013

Manila, Philippines—A week after Super Typhoon Haiyan hit, legitimate humanitarian aid has finally reached the devastated and resource-deprived Philippines. Thousands lined up as humanitarian workers gave out the first Facebook likes streaming in from around the world.

Many concerns have been voiced by survivors over a lack of supplies in overcrowded and understaffed hospitals and public shelters, as well as a sluggish and virtually nonexistent response from the local government. The most immediate response came from foreign nations, such as boxes of food and fresh water from the United States, in addition to several Osprey helicopters to access remote areas blocked by debris. The

British Ministry of Defense also announced last Monday that it would send an aircraft carrier and seven helicopters to Manila, the nation's capital. Still, concerns remain over whether or not the response was sufficient. However, the remainder of the international community has responded with full force to Haiyan via the Internet and the state-of-the-art social media network Facebook.

Haiyan, packing winds 3.5 times as strong as Hurricane Katrina, washed away entire towns on many islands when it arrived last week. The official nationwide death toll had increased to 2,360 by Friday morning. The deadly storm left more than 3,850 injured and at least 77 people reported missing.

Seventeen-year-old Facebook user Jessica Arnold commented: "OMG :(, cant belive. Soo sad but happy I can do mi part <3 (sic)."

Facebook founder Mark Zuckerberg announced early Monday morning that his network boasted thousands of community posts and status updates offering aid, best wishes, and prayers to the Philippines. One such post had already garnered 23,687 likes and 13,502 comments.

The initial posting on Facebook was of two stock photos depicting a crying American six-year-old girl and a damaged house from Hurricane Katrina overlapped with the words "Like/comment for victims of the Philippines flooding—ignore if you want them to die." Fifteen-year-old Sabrina James of Hartford, Connecticut, said, "I was looking through my news feed at pictures of my friends when I saw that post with the crying girl and I thought, 'Oh, jeez, look at this poor Indonesian girl crying. I need to like this right away, everybody else is,' so I clicked it knowing that I was doing the right thing."

"It's just like Kony 2012," said nineteen-year-old Jamal Arnav of Montreal, Canada. "Thanks to everyone on Facebook, we saved all the child soldiers in Africa. Now, we can save these people."

The Facebook "likes" reached Manila on Monday morning, bringing new hope and support to the victims, who have been plagued by malnourishment, dehydration, illness, and looting. Humanitarian workers set up several stations for thousands of survivors throughout the city, working tirelessly to give out the limited supply of "likes."

"There was this one guy who was just really beaten up . . . I mean, he was missing both of his arms, and we didn't really know how to give [the like] to him. I can't get his confused look out of my head," said Red Cross volunteer Eric Shuler. "Like" distribution was prioritized for crying women and children, as well as anyone in an American-themed shirt.

Added Shuler, "We know it's not the best, but it's the best we have. And I'm just glad we can help in any way we can."

Back in the United States, Facebook friends of Chinese national Hong Lei Ping noted that he had not liked any posts about Haiyan as of yet. "I mean, the guy is from the freaking country where this is all happening. How could that soulless monster not like this," questioned Facebook friend Gerald McDaniels. Ping could not be reached for comment.

Enjoy this article? Like us on Facebook!

The Tech-over

JUSTIN WISNICKI, Grade 10, Age 15. Oxbridge Academy of the Palm Beaches, West Palm Beach, FL, Donna Gephart, *Educator*

Five years ago, our government was overthrown. The people were angry over D.C. giving Miley Cyrus healthcare or something. They shut down the government, and the people revolted. The only documentation of any of these events are some status updates and a couple of Tumblr posts. Some people say it was when Oxford added the word "selfie" to the dictionary that the world started to decline. Our society, with young adults at the helm, turned to Silicon Valley to run our government. This sounded like a great idea at the time: It was a truly efficient area. We could have turned to Wall Street, but then we realized that was a terrible idea. Hollywood? Most people would prefer to log back into Myspace than let the people behind *Transformers* run the country.

Apple, Twitter, Google, and Vine were chosen, and now they wrestle for power and work to recreate life in their images. They fail to understand, however, that life is not a social network, and the people living it are more than "users."

Apple has made some great computers, but they are terrible at governing. The first thing they took over was the food supply (no, they did not ban all non-apple fruits). They did, however, work to make food more "stylish" and "cooler." Which is lovely, but prices have doubled. And they release a new refrigerator every nine months, making the current ones obsolete. If you don't pre-order a new fridge, all your food rots. Even if the new refrigerator looks exactly the same, it's "revolutionary." Also, iOven is rather glitchy.

Twitter hasn't done so well either. For example, this mere account of events is illegal. Why? It's more than 140 characters. That's right. Twitter gets a chance to create any law they so desire, and they choose "limit all written documents to 140 characters." Our new constitution: "We the People of the United States, in Order to form a more perfect Union, establish Justice, insure domestic Tranquility, provide for the c" That's it. To provide for what? Cornflakes? Cats? (Actually, it's probably cats.) They did tweet out some amendment summaries: "Amend2: right to bear arms #guns"

In school, students' essays must be fewer than 100 letters. This gives the teacher 40 characters to reply with a grade and few suggestions: #youregoingtobeheldback

It's tough conveying certain pieces of information through hashtags. #youwillneverwalkagain However, it's a great way to find trending life tragedies like your own. Did I mention success in life is determined solely based on how many followers you have? That actually is something that wasn't changed by the revolution . . .

The Census Bureau was taken over by the people who are indisputably the best at gathering personal information about everyone: Google. The tech company did have to make adjustments, though. For example, they're not used to having to go and collect information. Normally, people just give it to them (and then complain that the information they just gave them is in their possession).

Google also manages tax collection. They creatively attempt to disguise this program as a social network that they call GoogleMinus. They have a doodle for every type of tax. It's quite entertaining.

As far as television news goes, that's managed by the video-sharing site Vine. And all Vine videos must be under six seconds. Now every video in the United States must be under six seconds. Television news is now hilarious.

"Hello, I'm Brian Williams. Let's go to a repo . . ."

"We have a serious outbreak of a fatal disease that could kill you and your . . ."

"Thanks, we'll be back after these mess . . ."

You learn nothing! But it's fun to watch the anchors scramble to complete their sentences in the allotted time period.

Every Sunday Night, CBS airs their latest news magazine, *6-Seconds*. It starts with the signature "tick" of a stop watch and ends a few seconds later with the same sound.

Don't even get me started on Amazon firing missiles at customers who don't pay. And we believed their drones would be used for quicker delivery. All I know is, something must change before PSY becomes president based on YouTube views.

In Memoriam

SARAH MUGHAL, Grade 10, Age 16. Vestal Senior High School, Vestal, NY, Jeffrey Dunham, *Educator*

"Kettles whistle and cauldrons boil, time tides over and the world spins on; kings fall and queens are butchered, but the Muse remembers all."

These children's rhymes (though ridiculous in likening monarchy to boiling soup) are known to every person in all of Encautum, whether you ask the lowliest laborer or the Presiding Head of Parliament. It's a children's fable! It was written to comfort our story-loving offspring when the wind rattles the windowpanes, and the crops yield little but dust.

And yet, though the Muse has never been seen or heard, everyone knows she lives.

—*An Anonymous History of Encautum*, page 217

She had taken refuge behind the wooden walls of King Merlin's Inn for several days, her pursuers lost behind her. Well, inn was a relative word; it was actually three rooms crammed above a bookshop, rented out by the proprietor's wife, exasperated by her husband's inept sales skills.

A bookshop that sold titles like *Edgar Allan Poe's Children's Tales, The Medical Student's Guide to Witch Doctoring,* and *The*

Brothers Grimm: Tales of Thievery and Intrigue. But that was her fault, mostly. And now it was her task to set things right again.

Keen eyes surveyed the room before her: her pitted table with matching stool, her stiff cot, the peeling plaster walls, and the bumps in the wood floor. There was her squat candle, dripping and glowing serenely in its iron holder, and her window—a window that let in the bright sunlight and all the singing, the nuances of life in its bustling, carnival glory. Shouts and the laughter of children drifted in, the song of the city—"Queen Morgana's relics, only five shillins!" "Pendants to ward off wizards—two pence!" "Come in, come in, for a glimpse at the corpse of our great hero—MORDRED!"

That window into the marketplace was her peephole into the war front—a war not of blood and steel, but of wits and ink scrawling across pages—and she supposed what lay before her now was her armory, of sorts.

A glass inkwell stationed in the divot at the top of the desk—rotund like her grandfather's belly, capped with an iron lid wrought with grey swirls and leaves; it was filled halfway with ink dipped from the reservoir of the night sky, "borrowed" rather sneakily from the Night Palace (desperate times call for desperate measures). A soft white quill rested just below it, stiff barreled and dappled by sunlight—a gratuitous gift from the mountain owls of Nethand.

And finally, a bright-red leather-bound book, tooled in gold and clasped with bronze arrows.

Lying open on the oak desk and cloaked in shafts of sun and swirling, gleaming motes of dust, the stack of aged parchment waved tantalizingly at her. Shadows drew in, curling over the rest of the room as the candles in the wall lanterns burned out with a *wssshhhh*—nothing could take precedence over this moment, not one person. The blank page called to her—she could see how the ink would curl over the delicate leafs, how each word would slide snuggly onto the page, as if into a subtle slot made for it.

How can I muster the power these words must contain? she thought, despair suddenly dissipating her visions of curlicues and delicate sentences.

She sat down at the stool.

Taking a deep breath, the woman took up the quill, noting how quietly it slipped into her trembling fingers—as if it, at least, had total confidence in her abilities. Blinking the hot-ness in her eyes away, she reached out and flipped open the inkwell, the iron clinking against the glass with a satisfying tink! The ink within bobbed with an invisible tide, twinkling stars swimming just below the waves, much like the contents of her stomach.

The smell was intoxicating: faintly reminiscent of night breezes, evening dew, and lemon ice.

She watched the sharp nib pierce the surface of the ink, emitting ripples like waves in an ocean—the ocean of untapped dreams, ancient secrets and forgotten heroes just waiting to be put back into existence.

Ink was more than liquid pigment, she remembered. It was the life-blood of stories—and, she had been told, the substance that flowed through her veins in lieu of blood, so skilled was she with the pen, with the ways of words and story smithing. Why, even Devlin, with all of his teasing and doubting words, had sworn it to be true . . .

She squeezed her eyes shut, pinched her forehead; she had one last mission to complete, had too much at stake to dawdle and fumble. Let the dead sleep, with their grief and secrets untold, she told herself, stern and only slightly bitter. Tipping her chair, she held the nib up to the light to inspect it, becoming distracted yet again by the dripping ink—a blip of shadow held by a fraction, reaching and jerking lower and lower, nearly splattering the page.

With a start, she yanked the quill away from the book, sending the drop spattering into the wall—a new blemish on the spotted plaster. Stifling a groan, the woman dropped her head into her hand, propping her elbow on the table to steady it. Exhale, she remembered him saying—not Devlin, but her tutor, her wizard. Exhale, and let all the doubts and fears rush out with your breath—for it is those that still your pen and stem the flow of imagination, not anything nor anyone but yourself. If ink is the life-blood of stories, you are its master, its brain, and its creator. You must remember this.

She was procrastinating, she knew it. She simply was not cut out for the adventuring business—after all, hadn't she trained to give heroes advice, and not become one? Her hands were shaped to hold quills and stack books, not wield swords and fasten armor. They'd quipped about it countless times—how their dragon-wizard duo guided the company; how she was the brains and the magic handler; how he was the muscle, the knight to fight away beast and foe; how the girl was the distraction, their tiny spy to ferret out intelligence from markets and taverns and shadowy corridors.

How could all her years of studying histories and legends possibly help her survive long enough to put those skills to their final use?

With a sigh, she laid her head on the desk, snuggling her cheek into her arm as she stared at the page. A key to all worlds, yet holding nothing, she thought. A blank page is a powerful and utterly terrifying thing.

The thing was, it was a dangerous business to put pen to

paper. You did not make mere marks; oh no, it was something deeper, more ancient and powerful than that. A flick of your wrist, and a person, a hero, gasped into life. With a swirl of the pen, an entire realm came into being—breathing, pulsing, and more complex than even the creator could dream to fathom. The merest drop of ink combined with the bluntest quill on a stick of wood could create something that opened the door to magic, let power slip through the curtains of the universe—she knew it, she'd even done it, once (trapped, dragged to dungeons dank and filthy; peeling green-goblin skin, burning brands and blue tattoos, huddled against walls and torches flaring bright— what is it to know a fate, and not act?). It was magic, magic accessible to all and harming nobody, so long as it was pure and good.

And when a story was let loose into the world, it gained perhaps the most terrifying power of them all—it belonged to everybody. It became a part of the people, and the people saw themselves reflected in its words, its nuances and hero's face.

But she had more ability than that, and more responsibility—she, with all the power and skill passed on to her. In a trance, she could fly into emerald worlds beyond her imagination, embellishing and breathing life with the marks she left behind. She played Creator, though she was only a gnat in the entire scheme of the universe. She went diving for human secrets, exposed the gutters even as she drew them behind gauzy curtains on smoky stages. She sang haunting praises worthy of angels, and gifted all this to others—the knowledge and power she'd discovered, all for her people. To her, a quill was a kind of sword, albeit wielded on quite a different battlefield.

When she took up her arms, she had special purpose: to wage war for truth, to go to battle for these heroes, for these lessons to live on for people in their time of need. That was her responsibility. That was, in a sense, the price she paid for so much power and joy.

But now . . . everything she had admired, crafted, saved, and given—every story was dead, their heroes tampered and soiled, trod into the streets by her enemy of old. Hadn't she seen the defiled stories, and turned away repulsed? Who now would save the saviors, the ones through whose deeds taught the future their lessons? Who could possibly dare such a feat, when no one else could remember?

She knew the answer even as she asked the question. Devlin's words came back to her, rushing and filling all the dark holes in her heart. You could.

You could, you can, and you will. For deep down, yours is the courage of a thousand heroes and the wisdom of a thousand queens. You know that no one else will rise up to the fray. You shall be the one to step forward, and accomplish what the world needs to be done. It all—we all—fall for you, to assist you. Don't weep, love—even you know that no other can. Though it's as quiet as the summer breeze, your sacrifice will be the most sung of all.

It is up to you to set the legends straight—for if they remain muddled for much longer, it'll be for all of time. And all the brave deeds of heroes, lost . . .

He'd mistaken her tears as bitterness, not grief for him—the lovely fool.

His last words echoed in her mind, growing and encompassing everything, until she could not turn away—all the brave deeds of heroes, lost . . .

She remembered her youth; days spent gathering chickens' eggs and wandering in mountain fields, eyes hazy and mind far away. She remembered the space her parents left behind working jobs in the Capitol, her grandparents always trying to stand in for them. How dear they had been! The other children never were easy around her; they differed in taste and stature, she a wispy pint among towering giants who would barely attend school—enough to read and write and do simple sums. But her appetite was never satisfied; her friends were her heaps of books and the red woven rug in front of the hearth, along with the occasional tabby sidling up for warmth during long winter nights. She remembered lone adventures in swamps, scurrying around and poking under rocks, hoping to find some fairie in need of rescue—and then she could go adventuring, be more than just a spectator in one of her heroes tales.

She would be an extraordinary person at last.

But in its due course, tragedy struck their little family. For no sooner had she passed her 18th birthday, did her grandparents pass on to the next world.

Her parents hadn't taken time off for the funeral. It was the King's Vigil after all. What poor servant could miss the midnight feasts, attending lavish crowds of nobles reveling in washed streets?

She didn't care; she didn't need parents whose faces she could barely remember, whose only presence in her life was a bag of coins duly delivered every month.

She remembered how taken aback she'd been when she'd opened the door, after ten minutes of bearing incessant knocking, and come face to face with Devlin Heartswood—a squire in training, bouncing at her doorstep with black scabbard strapped to leather jerkin! And stranger yet, he'd known who she was, where she'd lived—and had, to her dismay, insisted on a place to stay for the night.

After him had come the little girl seeking her protection, Ava—the poor thing a bundle of arms and legs and hazel eyes, wrapped in a tattered sundress and wide, dirty rain boots—a child who could conjure a flame, or wind, or even a shard of ice in the palm of her hand.

Then the black, bright fire came razing at night, sending them running barely clothed into the mountains, and even as they fled, groups of mercenaries and assassins chased after them. A dragon with his wizard had flown across the sea to save her—and before she'd even realized, adventure came knocking for her.

But word had already reached the underground organization known only as the Breath (serving to bring a Breath of life to the True Mankind, and wash the earth of unnatural Demons sanctioning the practice of Magic). With the help of her companions, she'd escaped, and spent many years with them in other, fantastical worlds, learning things beyond her imagining, and battling just like the heroes she had read about all those years ago.

She'd not only become a hero; she'd grown up somewhere along the way too. And so had her heart, she realized, staring up into Devlin's deep blue eyes as they swept across the ballroom floor.

She watched, cheering behind her solemn mask as he was knighted by the king, ignoring the princess's radiant smile to grin at her with all the joy of life shining from his eyes. She'd rubbed the wizard's shoulder in silent comfort when, after hours of unrelenting searching, he'd throw his papers across the room to smash into elixirs and vanish in swirls of colored smoke. She'd sat on the dragon's shoulders and watched the sun come up. She'd mothered the girl as best as she could without knowing how mothers were, really.

Together, they'd made a new, patchwork family.

But stories rarely end in "happily ever after." Evil had overtaken them.

And there were none left to blame but herself, the one who

ought to have felt the enemy upon them.

She saw the future now; a world without magic falling in flames and smoke, the ashes left for evil to blow and scatter. The graves of the old stories spat on and serving as the foundation for a society built and totally controlled. She saw masses of the innocent and magical executed. Burnt. Obliterated.

She saw that no matter what, she stood to lose even more than she'd lost. And now she was all alone in the center of Legend, the ruins of the Capitol.

But that's not going to happen, she thought, shaking herself and bringing her senses back to earth. I will ensure that our sacrifice will be heard—ours will be the new legend for the people to draw hope from, the new story for the ages to hear echoing, the new gods to stand the rolling of time.

She turned her head to the ceiling, burning eyes resolute. If I couldn't save you or myself, then at least let me make us immortal. Let me make us the heroes of the ages—the ones who saved the heart of mankind.

She straightened up, allowed her head to bow in shame and mourning, of course. How could she forget their sacrifice so easily? She had accepted the burden, and if she could not bring herself to do it then she must think of all the others—the little girl, the aged wizard, her boy, her only love—and their final stand. The dead may be gone from us, she thought, vigor anew—but they never stop living in the hearts of the people they leave behind—and she must make sure that other people, too, knew that they were alive still.

The Breath would come after her for this, she knew. Yes, it would not be long before they came for her, as they had done over and over before. She grit her teeth, fiery ire trembling in her blood; the Breath had terrorized her and her kind for far too long—even they had no idea of the desolation that would come from altering legend. Those stories formed the beliefs, the very ideology of the people—how could it survive such an abrupt shake in foundation?

Who else was left besides her to fix the mistakes?

In that moment, the woman swore to herself a pact forged from the hatred, smoke, and blood given unduly to her: They may at last have her in their grasp, they may finally exterminate the last of their company, but she would make certain that they could do nothing about what she was going to unleash. She would weave a web so tightly around the Breath that they would be hardly tripping about before they were plunged into darkness, trapped and hanging for the rest of time.

Some stories could not be kept quietly whispered around hearths, could not be treated like secrets—those truths doomed to languish in the dark far away from people who needed it. And this was the Story, she knew it—the Story to change the world back. It had to be. Some things simply needed to be done, with no small amount of courage involved. And now, it was up to her, and her alone.

And so it was, in the heart of Legend, smiling in the face of her sacrifice, serene and peaceful to the depths of her heart, the woman—Muse, we can call her now—bent over the page, touching quill to paper and soul to ink, wrote:

Once upon a time . . .

Hungry House

GREGORY NAM, Grade 8, Age 13. Durham Community School,
Durham, ME, Sarah Duffy, *Educator*

The sky was an empty void, stretching from the distant mountains to the far cacti. Beneath me, the cold sand sifted between my toes, and the pebbles scratched at my calloused feet. All around me whistled the chilly night air, cutting right through my ragged clothes. To my left lay a cracked and sandy road, obviously long abandoned.

In all those days of wandering along the side of the road since the horrible crash, I had seen but one car speed along it's uncared-for pavement. A car whose driver was too preoccupied to notice the ragged man shouting and jumping to get his attention.

On the distant horizon, a light appeared. I shouted, though the effort tore at my sand-scratched throat. But it was not a car. The light came no closer, simply sitting there, perched upon the horizon.

Confused, I wandered slowly toward it, the black of the night nurturing my most paranormal and fearful superstitions. My subconscious told me to turn and run into the desert, to run until my legs give out, then crawl and die out of sight.

But my primitive side wasn't in control here. Despite my building horror, I continued toward the light. Slowly, the light cut away the shadows around me as well as my sense of fear. I raised a hand to shield my eyes. After days of living like a desert vulture, scrounging on roadkill and drinking from cacti, I was entirely unused to the light.

As my pupils adjusted, I reluctantly lowered my sand-caked hand. There, in all the beauty of its fluorescent lighting, was a small diner.

Part of me found it odd that a restaurant like this would be out here in the desert, but the other part of me was euphoric at the hope of another human face, of food, and perhaps some means of calling for help.

I increased my pace, too tired to run, but hurrying along as fast as I could. The name of the restaurant was a little funny: Hungry House. I shrugged the thought away. So it hasn't got a fancy name like MacRonalds; I just hope it has food.

As soon as I stepped into the diner, I was greeted by linoleum floors, fluorescent lights, and the smell of good old-fashioned burgers.

If I hadn't been able to look out the windows and see the desert outside, I would have believed I was in the middle of Chicago.

A stout waitress came over to me, her curly red hair pulled up in a bun. "Please, sir, take a seat." She gestured toward a window booth.

I wanted to ask her for some water, but my throat was so dry I simply croaked a short, sandpaper-against-sandpaper sound.

"That sounds like some dry throat you got there, sugar." She noticed. "I'll go fetch some water." I sank into my booth, grateful for some water. The waitress walked quickly back into the kitchen.

The restaurant had been abandoned when I walked in, but suddenly, someone slid into the seat across from me. "Hi!" he said cheerfully.

I simply stared at him. I didn't know this man.

He looked right back at me. "Mind if I sit here with you?"

Unsure how to react to this man's friendly manner, I just nodded.

He smiled and leaned back, putting his arms behind his head, stretching. "I could sure go for a good old cheeseburger, eh?" I nodded. Me too.

The door to the kitchen opened and shut as the waitress returned with my drink. "Here you go, sir," she said, setting down a cold glass of water down in front of me.

Unable to help myself, I seize the glass and pour the refreshing liquid down my parched throat. Ah, it feels heavenly to put water back in my body after so much had been sweated and cried out over the past few days.

After setting down the glass, I noticed the waitress had put down two bacon cheeseburgers on our table. An alarm went off in my head. Three things immediately hit me.

How on earth did she know to bring two cheeseburgers? I then wondered if she had perhaps seen my new acquaintance through the little window. That brought up the second issue. Why did the cheeseburgers have bacon on them? She may have heard my "friend" here mention cheeseburgers, but cheeseburgers take some time to cook, and he mentioned that mere seconds before she came out the door. I then thought, perhaps they had been preprepared? But then there is the third issue. Why was there bacon on the burgers? My favorite topping on burgers was bacon, but there was no possible way she could know that. Lucky guess, I thought as I reached for one. Who doesn't like bacon?

With those thoughts swirling in my head, I stuffed the burger in my mouth and ravenously chewed it into swallowable chunks.

The man watched me eat, then slid his plate over to me. "Have mine."

I looked at his untouched meal. "I couldn't."

"I insist."

Since I actually did want his food, I shrugged and devoured his burger. The waitress soon returned and asked, "Do y'all want anything else?"

I shook my head. "No, thank you." I pulled out my wallet, which luckily I had kept with me. "How much would that be?" She shook her head.

"S'all right, honey. It's on the house."

I looked at her for a second then shrugged and put my wallet away. "Thank you."

She looked at me. "Thank you, dear."

And with that she turned and walked back into the kitchen. I got up to go when my friend came over, and he said, "Come, walk with me."

That was such a strange thing to say, that suddenly all my suspicions and fears resurfaced. Cautiously, I decided to accept.

"Sure." I said slowly.

He nodded and gestured toward the door. Before long I was back under the moonless sky, with the cold sand on my feet and the breeze at my back.

The glow of the diner faded until it was nothing more than a comforting glow on my back, spreading in front of me and casting, strangely enough, no shadows.

My friend was talking to me about the sky and the stars and what else lay in the heavens, but I hardly paid any attention. Everything about the whole incident seemed very strange to me. Through my thoughts, I heard a pause in the stranger's voice, then the question,

"Do you ever think about death?"

I whirled on him, all my questions exploding out of me:

"Who are you? Where am I? What were you doing there? Did you know that waitress? What happened at that diner?" He smiled slowly and asked a teasing question that suggested he already knew the answer.

"What diner?"

I gaped at him. I pointed. "The one ov-" I stopped.

It was gone. When I hadn't been paying attention, the light had faded away. The diner had vanished clean off the face of the earth.

I turned back to the stranger. "What the heck is going on here?"

He had a sad tinge to his voice. "That place, it existed purely to make your last experience a good one."

I backed away from him.

"Ar-are you going to kill me?" He returned my look.

"Don't be ridiculous, I have no intention of harming you whatsoever."

Staggering back, I tripped on something. I turned to see what it was and choked on a near scream.

A human body lay sprawled in the sand. A corpse by the look of it, surely only a dead man would rest in that position, crawling feebly toward some unseen goal.

"Wh-who? What?" I jittered, bouncing across sentences and leaving behind a trail of incomprehensible words. I shot a frightened look at the man, waiting for an answer.

He simply turned and said, "Come on. Let's go."

But I wouldn't. "No."

He turned back at me. "No?" I took another step back.

"This man needs to be buried." I reached for him. "No," protested the man, and he grabbed my arm.

"Let me go." I said through gritted teeth. "Have you no respect for the dead? If I can't bury him, at least let me see if I can identify him!"

The man let me go and stared at me in surprise. "Really?" he said in an incredulous voice. He suddenly laughed. "Why you are most ignorant! Go ahead and identify your dead fellow!"

I looked at him. "Do I know this man?" He gestured toward the body.

Hesitantly, I stooped down and grabbed the stiff, cold body and flipped the corpse over. This time I did scream. The face of the dead man on the ground was my own.

Tears in my eyes, I looked up at the man. "What is this?"

He sighed. "This is never easy to say, which is why I tried to let you figure it out yourself." He took a deep breath. "My friend, you're dead and have been dead for the past several hours."

I backed away. This man was obviously crazy. I then looked back down at the face I saw in the sand and wondered, *Am I mad as well*?

"You died the instant you saw the first ray of light from the Hungry House. Of thirst and hunger, of loneliness and depression. The diner was a heavenly simulation, shall we say, for you to experience happiness before you had to go, but whenever a wish for you was granted, all you felt was suspicion." The man continued. "And now my brother," he reached out a hand, "it's time for us to go."

Tears cut through my sand-caked cheeks. "I-I don't want to go!"

"It's okay," he said, and a calm, confident smile stretched across his handsome face. I hesitantly reached out a hand, then drew it back.

"It's okay," he repeated, smile never wavering. Shaking, I reached out and took his hand.

The pain and grief, anger and suspicion, evil and spite that I'd felt, all melted away. I was calm and confident, just as the muscular youth before me. He turned and led me into a new light, and the welcome and the light of the Hungry House, yet, somehow more pure now, purer than anything on Earth could be. I followed my friend into the light, and . . . and . . .

I was home.

The Ghost Singer

MAIREAD KILGALLON, Grade 8, Age 13. Rippowam Cisqua School, Bedford, NY, Brooks Eleck, *Educator*

Shh, now. Can you hear it? Don't cry.
The voice?
Sleep, my angel.
For it lurks, in every corner.
Come home,
every shadow.
Come and rest.

You must not trust it.

As so many have done, and met their dooms.

It is the Quietus, what has ravaged Scathen, a place known as Africa in ancient times. Apparently, the land used to be covered with millions of trees, all of which were so big that you could lie beneath them and be shaded from the eye of the Sky-fire, which incessantly stares down on the earth. Sometimes I look to the dark horizon and wonder what it's like in Lunem, under the Nightsilver. There are two sides of the world: Scathen, where it is always day, and Lunem, where it is always night. Lunem is infected with the Quietus as well, but that is all anyone in Scathen knows about the other part of the earth.

The Skyfire and the Nightsilver, once known as the Sun and Moon, shine on each side of the planet, and do not move as they once did. No one knows why, just like no one knows why the Quietus began.

But it began. And that's all that matters now.

Plants are the only thing that we can eat now, and they are becoming scarce. Most of Scathen is one endless desert with cracked earth and relentless heat. There are small villages here and there, where a few people struggle to survive if they haven't already come down with the Quietus.

Unlike any other disease, the Quietus became a pandemic in a matter of hours. No one knows where it started or how. All anyone knows about it is that it takes residence in the brain of the victim, and exists as a soothing, irresistible voice that says to sleep, to simply stop living. And the victim obeys. So, suddenly, people were dropping dead on the streets, while at home, drifting off to sleep and never waking up. The few who are able to fight to remain conscious for a while say that they cannot disobey It, It holds power over them and they must do as It asks. That's all they ever have time to say. The Quietus is also unique because it travels not only through the air and physical touch, but by sight. If you make eye contact with a person who is infected, the voice takes residence in your mind as well.

There are whole villages that are seemingly deserted, but inside there are hundreds of Quietus victims, some dead, some still just sleeping. Very rarely do they remain conscious for more than a couple of hours before they are infected, and victims of the disease can remain sleeping for up to a week before dying, if given the proper care.

Though, as far as I know, proper care isn't something that's abundant. Many people have become nomads now, trying not to stay in one place for too long, hoping to keep from catching the disease, even though they know it's impossible. Humanity has resigned itself to extinction by now, mostly just waiting out in caves, hoping to be the last to go. I myself am a nomad, I left my village after it was ravaged by the Quietus. I never had any family, so it was easier for me to accept the fact that everyone there was dead. In fact, it was easier to accept that they were dead than the fact that I wasn't.

I was in the village when the first person got it. Collapsed on the way to the well. I was on the scene, and even made eye contact with the victim. I was sure I was going to catch the Quietus as well, so I sat down in the grass and cried, waiting for the voice to come, to tell me to sleep. But it didn't.

After hours of waiting, I realized that it wasn't going to come. I had gotten lucky. Maybe I actually hadn't looked into the person's eyes after all. So, unbelievably happy, I ran back to my little hut at the edge of the village. But I had forgotten that the whole town was probably infected by then. When I was reaching for my front door, a hand shot out and grabbed my ankle, and when I looked down, it was a small child, barely awake, looking at me sleepily.

"I'm scared," the child had mumbled. "Mommy, sing to me. Mommy, please."

I was frozen, staring at the child, half-expecting to crumple to the ground now that someone infected had physically touched me. I waited again, and like last time, the voice didn't come. Not knowing what to make of this strange occurrence, I looked down toward the child again, who was straining to stay conscious. "Sing to me, Mommy," the child murmured again.

Well, I thought to myself, the kid is already touching me, won't hurt if I touch him a little more, right? So I gathered the child into my arms and brought him inside. I sat down on my little bed and held the child in my lap, trying to think of a song to sing. I was racking my memories when one surfaced: a memory of a blazing fire and laughter and song, when people told stories and shared thoughts and experiences with each other, looking at one another and touching freely. A memory that wasn't even mine. But it held a song, and it was the only one I could think of. It went like this:

Under the mountains and over the clouds
A place far away of which travelers laugh
Off in the distance
Where the sun is so warm
And the children all play
From the dusk till the dawn

The clouds are of white
And the grasses so green
There flies the sparrow in song
So fair to be seen
So come now my children
Stop resting your heads
Play long and happy now
Till all's long and dead.

And when I looked down, the child had died.

So, wiping the tears off my face, I had given the child the most decent burial I could, packed up all my belongings, and set off for the desert.

That was five years ago. Now, I still have never gotten the Quietus, and have gone to the outskirts of every village I come across and sung to the dying people there as I sang to the child. I have even made a name for myself among the few remaining people who aren't infected in Scathen. They call me the

Ghost Singer, since I never stay after I sing to the people. Some have actually come to take the name seriously, thinking I am a ghost, since I can't get the Quietus. The only explanation for which is simply this: I am immune.

There must be something special about me, maybe in my blood or brain, that can resist it. I haven't had any research done or anything, I doubt there are even enough people educated enough to do that sort of thing anymore.

I just do what I do because I don't want the people with the Quietus to feel how that child did. Scared, alone, crying for his mommy. So that is why I sing to them. To let them know that no matter what, they aren't alone, and that their mommy loves them, and that they're going somewhere that's better than here.

I am the Ghost Singer. And my song goes on.

The Search for Intelligence Beyond the Fine-tuned Universe

JAE WOO JANG, Grade 12, Age 17. International School Manila, Taguig, The Phillipines, Andrea Thompson, *Educator*

I bade farewell to Voyager 1 the last time I caught a glimpse of it on the pages of *National Geographic*. After four decades, it was still a golden-winged moth far beyond the ebb of its glory days. Voyager will continue to tear through the exigency of darkness and toward the promise of light after completing its mission. A decade from now, Voyager will cease transmitting information back to earth and will continue to drift toward the labyrinths of the cosmos. It would be the last we see of it and the vestige it carries of the good in each of us and the evil into which we often relapse. But at Voyager's core is the Golden Disc, and into that immensity of space, it will unravel and transmit, if intelligent life exists out there that would listen, through radio waves, our story, our images and languages, our history, or at least some of it, though lamentably devoid of the imprints of the majority whose lives were squandered in quiet desperation.

Yet Voyager and the Golden Disc are not just a wedge of a life lived on our planet, a repository of intelligence, or our penchant for self-destruction. They are also a parcel of our insatiable appetite for wanderings and perilous journeys and the endless quests for understanding. In the complex thicket of the cosmic haystack, Voyager broadcasts our lives to those who can hear it, and for four decades since it was launched to search for lives other than our own, its radio signals aimed at every possibility, we have yet to receive a rejoinder. Is life so rare and unique that we can hear only our own voices, our own prayers and lamentations?

That the universe is fine-tuned, built only for us, paving the way for our species to thrive in dominion, brings a lot of assurance for many, as it substantiates the promise it holds about our unique place in the cosmos. Yet it also implies that life could be rare. If the universe were fine-tuned for life, it means life abounds. This springs upon the claims that the fundamental constants in our universe have been exquisitely fine-tuned to a precision laying the foundations for the development of life [1]. Thus, on these intrinsic values, scientists claim, depend our evolutionary history and future. Contentions abound that the mathematical and astrophysical constants observable in the universe remain naturally attuned for life—at least the life that exists on earth as the laws of physics, which account to hundreds of factors that hold the universe together cannot be merely attributed to chance. To put it more simply, fine-tuning implies that the constants in physics, the laws of nature and the preliminary conditions present during the inception of the universe were laid out perfectly to allow life to emerge. Hence, the opportune amalgamations of the laws of nature—electromagnetism, gravity, and the nuclear force binding protons and neutrons together in an atom—must have paved the way for complex life to evolve.

The mathematician Gottfried Leibniz posed an analogous question: What would our universe look like if certain factors in astrophysics were a bit different? This conundrum had motivated many scientists to explore the specific cosmological constant that necessitates the emergence of life on earth. The theoretical physicist Brandon Carter stresses that our universe had been initially fashioned, or 'fine-tuned,' to lay down cosmological foundations for life to thrive, reminiscent of the conditions present in our planet. This argument on fine-tuning is substantiated by astrophysicist Martin Rees, [2] who put forth the significant constants and the Standard Model of particle physics. This considers the relationship between the intensity of the gravitational force, electromagnetisms, space time, and the binding force of nuclei. Rees emphasizes that if any of these initial constants were slightly off of bounds, then our universe would have developed very disparately—hence, theoretically, life would not have emerged. These specific values seem almost impossible to replicate, as the relationship between electrically charged particles and the gravity that play upon them, also known as the N-variable, should be 39 orders of magnitude stronger than the gravitational force in the universe. Had a minute difference between the two opposing forces existed, stars would have collapsed, and life would not have existed. We can also compare this to building a castle using a deck of cards—if these cards were slightly off an acclivity, then the whole stack-of-card castle would immediately collapse. The same laws of physics apply to us and the atoms that built the flotsam of life.

The problem with the fine-tuning argument, however, is that it basks in arrogant generalizations about the universe we barely understand. It also blindly argues for an orderly universe using only constants and parameters that, when altered, will be difficult to test, as we cannot replicate the immensity of events and factors that unraveled the face of our universe. The evolution of the universe and life on earth fall within the bounds of these 'fine-tuned' parameters, and it is safe to say that life has fine-tuned itself within these requirements and not the other way around. In addition, as these constants and parameters if altered cannot be duplicated in a laboratory setting, it is absurd to assume that if the cosmological constants are disparate, life as we know it would not have evolved. What that will result in is most probably a universe with different constants strung together by diverse laws of physics. Proponents of fine-tuning failed to consider the implications of their arguments on evolutionary biology and the volatile events that pose threats to life as a whole. If fine-tuning were true and our place in the cosmos were determined as unique, then even a slight change in the level of carbon dioxide in the atmosphere would have not resulted in the decimation of life, and an asteroid impact would not have caused the end of the dinosaurs' domination on earth.

Now, if our universe was so fine-tuned for life, why can't we find any other life besides our own? The continuous failures in our search for life, or in the desperation of waiting for an alien life to reveal itself to us, indicate one proof—life is not as abundant as we think. Our knowledge about the cosmos remains incomplete—and limiting our views on the formation of intelligent life within the constraints of our understanding will only thwart the development of knowledge needed to search for life outside our own.

Beyond the fine-tunings that its supporters preach as manifest in the universe, the laws of nature that replete our planet and beyond it unveil random events: The intermittent, unpredictability of volcanic eruptions, decimated matters in space finding their ways to the bosom of the earth, climatic changes and vacillations in ocean temperatures that affect our weather patterns. These arbitrary occurrences and the changes in the environment unfolding after another, whose causes are unexplainable, are in fact spurred by chance. The collapse of the molecular clouds, the mass of our terrestrial planet and other astrobiological factors that paved the way for the emergence of life on earth are filters through which earth had uniquely winnowed in order to host sentient creatures. It's as if a billion-faced dice is rolled and for a single factor, change occurred in our planet in which each face accounts to a different set of outcomes. This dice is then rolled a billion times to reveal the results of minute factors. Hence, the probability, the sequence of random events, of the emergence of earth is almost, to an extent and possibly, as improbable as one over a billionth billion chance. Stephen Jay Gould explored this idea of randomness in evolution in his book *Punctuated Equilibrium*, in which he contends that evolution, based on his studies of fossilized ancient snails, occurs at punctuated patterns of change when there lacks a necessity for change. [3] This contrasts with the Darwinian gradualism in which evolution is gradual and constant. Either way evolution occurs, it is often characterized by randomness, necessity, and unpredictability—hallmarks of adaptation and coping mechanisms. If biology were fine-tuned, life wouldn't have achieved complexity through a gradual, sometimes punctuated, and excruciating process of change. The fine-tuning argument, therefore, is too deterministic in a universe woven by chance, volatility, and randomness.

Chaos theory in mathematics offers a more acceptable explanation of how the intricate and immense strings of results form minute fortuities. [4] It posits that initial causations, as for instance, rolling two marbles at the same point of origin using the same amount of force and other variables, can lead to different outcomes, as the marbles land at two different places. This refutes the argument of determinism, the core of the fine-tuning argument, often misinterpreted by theologians who claim that our universe had to be initially fine-tuned for life here on earth—or else the changes in the astrophysical constants would have greatly altered the fate of the species. But the essential message upon which chaos theory stands is that outcomes are random—even if change spurred from a definite goal, results fall through disparately. In fact, the very essence of which this theory is founded upon is the idea of unpredictability. From this basis, our view of the cosmos must lean toward the idea that the emergence of life occurred from chance resulting from astrophysical and astrobiological factors.

This means that an insignificant phenomenon can carry substantial effects. A careful consideration of this holds importance in our understanding of the origin of life as understanding how life came about on earth remains an invaluable aid in our quest for other intelligent life beyond ours in a mysterious universe.

Our understanding of how life began in the midst of chaos originated with the Big Bang that transpired approximately 13.7 billion years ago. [5] The inception of the universe came with the expansion of space and time. All that amalgamation of energy, like a pressurized fireball, spewed force in all directions, creating what we now know as matter, energy, time, and the laws of nature. Although why this transpired remains unknown, we know that from this, gas was dispersed, molecular clouds and the first stars began to emerge amidst the ghastly darkness of the universe. Dense clouds of matter and the first-generation stars swirled like a cauldron of boiling milk within a billion years into the cosmic expansion. [6]

Molecular clouds often hover like giant amorphous bubbles that brandish the reminiscences of stellar dusts and matter as dense as a hundred thousand magnitude of a sun's mass. However, on rare occasions, probably by chance, these molecular clouds are prone to danger. Many first-generation stars, which usually were 100 to 300 times bigger than our sun, often collapse from the supernova explosions that discharge matter across the galaxies; if unfortunate, some of these materials splinter through a molecular cloud for it to fall apart. From here, the molecular cloud should surpass a series of differential rotation, turbulences, and an excessively high concentration of dense matter. [7]

This shows that the universe is chaotic—destruction of matters leads to another obliteration of matter. These cosmic wraths of gargantuan scale may eradicate the earth or the solar system within minutes. However, nature's debacle may pave the way for other beginnings, and its randomness may present another opportunity. But most of the time we are left to bask under the blankets of unknowing.

The nuclear fusions that occurred within the scorching hot cores of the first-generation stars transmuted light elements such as helium and hydrogen into heavier elements such as iron and titanium. [8] These count as important processes in that some of these elements are essential to the composition of our sun and our earth. [9] When that star exploded, these elements scattered across the universe, transporting new heavier materials that earthly life requires. This debris may have landed in the depths of the gravitational collapse of a molecular cloud that sometimes generates small enough fragments of accretion disk, later shaped into a solar system. In the case of earth, this happened approximately 9 billion years after the Big Bang. [10]

The area around the newly emerged star, an accretion disk, feeds onto the development of the protostar—the early stages of a sun. As this infant star emits light for existence, its gravitational energy paves for an eternal increase of its core's temperature, which we can often deem as the sun's age—the older it is, the hotter its core becomes. This is in fact critical to the development of life on earth, as the primary role of the sun is to produce elements that enrich the composition of its planets. The hotter the core, the heavier the elements produced by the nuclear fusion. Thus, carbon burns to neon and oxygen to sulfur.

A variety of dust particles and nearly formed heavier elements shroud the accretion disk with dense matters. The accumulation of this dust stimulates static electrical forces to enable the formation of tiny asteroids. Some of these materials may get drafted out into the universe, while some may merge into many tiny planetesimals, which later may collide, by chance, with others to fuse together into terrestrial planets in a star system.

After the sun developed its own magnetic force, which is known as a T-Tauri stage, the planets have finally established their orbital routes. Following this, the heavy rock bombardment on earth, which is hypothesized to account for the formation of the moon, had gradually waned approximately 9 billion years after the Big Bang. [11] From here, the earth developed its own atmosphere through the accumulation of nitrogen, carbon dioxide, hydrogen, and other gases that were the result of the evaporation from the impact of planetesimal and earth. Simultaneously, the silicate material in the earth's mantle are noted to release the trapped H_2O onto the crust as the ice in the comets melted from the impact against the earth, delivering water and creating vast oceans, factors significant in the emergence of earthly life. [12]

The crude steps enumerated above are actually the result of several billion filters and chances that in some gash of luck we had been so fortunate enough to thrive upon. Out of chance, the supernova explosion may not have occurred near enough for it to disrupt the molecular clouds. If such external threats did not exist, the collapse of the molecular cloud would have been very rare, which in turn could stifle the formation of an accretion disk. The filter continues on as the asteroid belts or the small planetesimals that have been completed destroyed themselves into debris, owing to excessive collision against each other, while some planetesimals may have burnt into the wraths of the sun's gravitational pull, never merging to become a sizable planet to create its own magnetic field and its atmosphere. Hence, to a certain degree, the emergence of life heaves its chances on the timing of each factor. [13]

The enigma of the emergence of life, however, still needs to be deciphered, as we delve deeper into the biological processes that lead to biogenesis. We observe that protein is the most essential building block to almost all life; it cements our prototype, the manual instruction book of us, in the sequence of DNA. Amino acids are vital constituents in the production of this protein, and scientists can trace the most simplistic formation of DNA from its basic composition of protein. Yet there is also a possibility that other life forms may not share the same DNA as ours.

Based on our current knowledge of the earth, we have created a gauge, an alternative framework, that identifies possible habitable zones in other solar systems. But efficient it may seem, the farther we may stray from our endeavors to seek intelligent life. We must acknowledge that the evolution of intelligent life-forms depends on their necessity and most often a rare occurrence of accident. The fact that our ancestral herbivore hominids during the late Miocene, for example, chose to partake of carcasses of dead animals during harsh changing conditions allowed the brain to grow as a result of ample protein intake. And possibly from countless dangers posed by other predators, our ancestors might have found the necessity to critically use their brain to evade threats. Hence, randomness is manifest in the emergence of intelligent life-forms, which then adds another degree of rarity of sentient existence in our universe, as such necessity may not easily occur. [14]

But what does this volatility and randomness mean for our search for intelligent life beyond our turf? And what does this imply about the existence of life in the universe?

The necessity for intelligence must be present in the gradual development of higher thinking. In the case of humans, random accidents and unintended results shaped human intelligence, the one that best suited earth. However, with an extraterrestrial life, nature's demands and the environmental factors may affect the type of intelligence acquired. Chaos theory insinuates that the same or even similar results of two occurrences are rather rare, thus, even our framework for the possibility of life will get trampled upon by other cosmological facts that are to unravel in the future. All of these sequences of random accidents substantiates the rarity of intelligent life and the different outcomes of these accidents.

Hence, Voyager 1 drifts toward these accidents, hoping to stumble upon life that can discern the longings of humanity trying to find just a streak of it in another form. But what if a lone hunter in the darkness of a forest hears only his own cry? We search for a needle in a haystack, but what if it's not the needle we are looking for? In our search for intelligent life in the universe, we have to look beyond the needle, maybe beyond the haystack of our understanding of who we are—and more of what we're not.

To see footnotes, please go to **www.artandwriting.org/galleries**.

The Thing About Apples

LILY GORDON, Grade 9, Age 14. Bard High School Early College, New York, NY, Adrian Agredo, *Educator*

The thing about apples is they've got this red skin on the outside. And if you didn't know any better, you might think the inside would be just as red. But as soon as your teeth sink through the surface of the skin and you taste the sweet acid juice dripping onto your tongue and you take your mouth away, you see how white those insides are.

You learn to hate apples real quick. In fifth grade, your classmates call you "apple." They shout it at you on the playground, chant it over and over until sweet acid apple juice filled your eyes. They say it twisted and ugly and so many times that you swear never to eat another apple again.

And then, as you're brushing your teeth one night, you catch your reflection staring back at you through the mirror. Now this mirror is ugly and poor. It's got black ugly blotches at the corners growing and swelling up like diseases. And it's dirty, like it hasn't been washed in a while. And it's got a dent that distorts your mirrored face.

And you look at how red your skin is. You're so sure how red it is. It's so red that you think that the insides should be red, too. So you take your left wrist to your lips and bite your teeth down hard. But your teeth slide down and leave only light indentations of teeth marks. And now your mind's fixed so firmly on your inside colors that you'd do just anything to see it. And then you see dad's pocketknife sitting idly next to the toothbrushes and toothpaste. And before you think too long or hard, you grab it and send it deep into your wrist. And the apple skin peels away and shows the white bone. And you start screaming.

Mom comes in and sees the knife in your wrist and almost starts screaming, too. And you're not screaming because it hurts. You're screaming because of that white color inside you.

And the doctor at the Indian Health Service building gives you only half the normal amount of painkillers because he's fooled by your red skin and doesn't know how the white insides are exploding with apple pain.

And as the doctor stitches up your wrist, you stare at his white skin and white hair and white coat. "How'd you get to be so white?" you ask.

The doctor's eyes never even leave your wrist. "Hold still," he says.

Then you're sitting in the passenger seat of the old run-down family car. It barely had enough gas to get you home, but it'll have to make do until Mom's wallet isn't so thin.

Mom doesn't say anything. She's staring at the road. Her fingers are wrapped so tightly around the wheel that her red knuckles almost turn white. Minutes go by and she doesn't say a word. And then, "How'd you get that knife in your hand?" she says. She says it real quiet, like barely above a whisper. And her voice is almost as tight as her fingers on the wheel.

You think of the boys and girls at school shouting "apple." Of how they'd say it over and over until you could still hear it even after they had stopped, until that word covered your arms and legs, coating you bright red over white fleshy insides.

You look hard out the window, staring at the pine trees hugging the sides of the road. Pine trees all look the same. They have brown bark and green leaves. Behind those trees lives a river. You learned about that river in class. How over time, the rushing water eroded the rocky sides of the river, making the cut where the river lived bigger and bigger.

Mom's driving is steady. It doesn't curve. It stays perfectly straight and follows the yellow dotted lines carefully, like how she cut out the little coupons from magazines. And she hasn't moved her body a centimeter when you say, "I did it." Her body stays just the same, and her driving is just as steady.

But when you glance up at the rear-view mirror, you see the single wet shiny crooked line down her face, snaking like the river from the corner of her right eye to the line of her jaw. It looks like a scar made of tears. And you imagine that scar river on her face slowly eroding the rocky layers of her face, biting through Earth's crust. You watch as the tears wear away at her cheeks, forming a groove on the side of her face. You watch as the tears take away red skin sediments deep inside her skull, leaving the brain and insides exposed. But she was all red like rubies and bleeding diamonds.

A Series of Crowded Places

ASHLEY ISRAEL, Grade 12, Age 18. Fine Arts Center, Greenville, SC, Sarah Blackman, *Educator*

I.

Imagine you are x and your father is y and your ex-wife is z. Multiplying y and z yields a string of disappointments—a mug of coffee gone cold, a late birthday card, an unscented bar of yellow soap. Dividing x into its fine and separate parts results in variable (blank). Is the blank space you? Is it the line at a metro station or a flooded snowstorm in December? Is it a Wednesday church service, is it a mall of electrified teenagers, is it a circle of lit cigarettes by a newspaper fire? Is it me? Is it God? Is it anything at all?

II.

A man walks into a bar. Joining him are a pair of soldiers, a nuclear physicist, a dog, a farmer, a priest, a horse, a grasshopper, a homosexual, a couple of peanuts, a cheating husband, and God. It is a noisy bar.

III.

In July I sat on the steps of my apartment and counted women. The boys on the neighboring stoops hollered and brought up their frequent sex. The women marched forward, bags thumping at their waists. I looked closely at the women's eyes—how they squinted just slightly at the boys' sounds, or how the lashes stuck together at the lids' close. I waited for reciprocation, for gratification toward my lack of effort. But the women ignored me, isolated their eyes from their bodies and looked forward, stiff and unconcerned with whatever was around them.

Escape

JUSTIN GAINSLEY, Grade 8, Age 13. The Blake School-Blake Campus, Hopkins, MN, Stacy Swearingen, *Educator*

Hawk and I decide that on the count of three, we would sprint. "One . . . two . . ." I mutter in a shaky voice, "three." We sprint. Only looking at the fence, not behind us, not at the guards. We have 50 yards to the fence when we hear yelling. The guards fire a shot. They miss, hitting the ground in front of us. With 25 yards to go, the sirens go off. The deafening noise blasts into my ears as I catapult my legs forward. More guards are shooting, missing, but very close behind.

Why am I here? I ask this rhetorical question every day. I can't believe that I am trying to escape, sprinting my way toward the fence. The punishment lasts three generations, so when my great-grandpa questioned our leader, he didn't know that he would be putting his children and their children in this horrible place as well. It's been my whole life, 19 years of confinement, doing slave work here in this labor camp. They murdered each of my family members who attempted to escape, protest, or stop working. We are located somewhere in North Korea, but I do not know where. We are told that we are located close to the DMZ, but we don't know what to believe. Every day I watch my very own friends get shot and murdered on the shooting stand. We all watch in despair, hoping and wishing that we are not next, while knowing that could be soon to come.

Ten yards to the fence, a bullet hits my right calf. The immense pain scolds my insides, an ocean of cries is pushed through my leg, up into my body. No words can describe this pain, but right when I am about to give up, Hawk grabs on to me. He is running, pushing us forward, getting us past the fence. I remember the days of just working, when I sat in my dirty cell, a dark, lonely, concrete structure with a toilet and a small mattress. I dreamed of escaping like this every day. I told myself that I would sprint out the north fence opening, at 2 a.m. when the prison guards switch shifts. The fence is a rusty, barbed-wire death trap, but I hoped getting to the opening at the right time, I would be able to crawl through the gap with minimal injuries. He also had the constant desire to escape, and reveal to the world what this horrible place contains. We have always been friends, and we always have been planning together our strategic way out. He had lived in the cell next to me, making it easy to communicate. After months finalizing our elaborate plan, we had decided that we would make the attempt on August 14, nine days from the finishing of our plan. We still have no idea what the world looks like, smells like, tastes like, or feels like, but we visualize the moment we reach safety. We are going to succeed, I told myself, or at least die trying.

When we reach the fence, prisoners are running toward us, trying to help the guards to protect their own safety. The sirens are blasting, guards are running and shooting, with a desire to bring us to a stop. I climb under the fence, razor wire tearing into my skin, ripping me into pieces. It feels like I am in a blender, being cut and sliced, a horrible feeling. At this time, I remember the nine days of waiting for this in despair. Just a few hours ago, Hawk and I pretended to work, so guards wouldn't suspect anything awry. After some time passed, we migrated closer to the north fence opening, pretending to take a break. "How long?" Hawk had whispered to me. I saw him sweating and showing nervousness, because both of our lives were soon to be at risk. I glanced at my dirty, partially destroyed watch. "1:45. Let's just prepare ourselves for some commotion," I replied. Off into the distance, I remember seeing the shadows of two guards leaving their post. "Hawk!" I had yelled in a whisper, "They are changing early. We've got to move."

It is 1:46, and I am through the fence first, bullets still being shot. I worry that I am losing blood too rapidly. I need to put pressure on the leg wound. Hawk continues helping me through the pain as we run. I am getting light-headed, but I push on. After around an hour, I collapse to the ground from loss of blood and unfathomable pain.

It is still dark, but I see Hawk reclining to my left. He is glancing at me with a big smile. I haven't seen a smile in 14 years, since before my family was killed. We are resting by a pond, and I see my right leg wrapped in a tight bundle of rope and fabric. "You fell about 3 miles away from the camp. I carried you another half a mile to this pond, where I got you patched up," Hawk murmurs. I decided that I would persevere through the pain, and keep walking toward the glowing city lights many miles in the distance. I am lathered in mud, in severe pain, and we don't know where we are going, but anything is better than spending any more time in that horrible camp. I check my watch, 4:47 a.m. It has been three hours since we left, and guards won't be too far behind us. Hawk suggests that we attempt to run until the sun rises, to get us close to the city we see in the distance. I agree, but only because I need medical attention soon.

At around 10 a.m., we arrive in an unfamiliar city called Paju. We made it to South Korea, and we will soon be able to share our story, and my pain will vanish away.

Fracking Into the Future

RYAN CHUNG, Grade 8, Age 13. Manhasset Middle School,
Manhasset, NY, Eric Shapiro, *Educator*

Did you know that in a few years, the U.S.'s oil production
may exceed that of Saudi Arabia? (Chris Nelder) Oil companies
often advertise that this will lead to energy independence and
more reliable fuel for the U.S. economy. However, much of this
oil, unbeknownst to many, is unconventional—such as shale
oil. Shale oil is made into synthetic oil and gas, and is later
refined. Many hazards for workers and communities related to
the extraction of these crude oils exist. Although the extraction process can have a negative impact on general health and
environmental conditions, pipeline deals are secured years before the plans are released to the public; some deals secured as
early as 2007 are currently in effect in the U.S. ("Enbridge and
BP") Some people have expressed their doubts, while others
have shown support for this method.

Varying Viewpoints
Fracking, or hydraulic fracturing, is used to extract oil from
rocks beneath the earth's surface by forcing open fissures
with a liquid consisting of water, sand, and about 600 other
chemicals, such as uranium, formaldehyde, and hydrochlo-
ric acid. ("What Goes In and Out of Hydraulic Fracturing")

Creating fracking wells and producing other unconventional oils, including shale oil, an unconventional oil produced from oil shale, can "boost [the] U.S. economy $2,000 per household [annually]," according to Paul Brown in "Fracking to Boost U.S. Economy $2,000 per Household—Report." (Responding to Climate Change) In what is called the "unconventional oil and gas revolution," the U.S.'s unconventional oil production from oil sands and shale is rapidly burgeoning. Halliburton reports, "Over the past six decades, hydraulic fracturing has helped deliver more than 600 trillion cubic feet of natural gas to American consumers, the product of more than 1.1 million separate and successful [international] fracturing applications during that time." The CEO and chairman of Exxon-Mobil, Rex Tillerson, said, "I think we have to deal in facts. The assertions that our opponents make—why don't you ask them to produce some facts, produce something? I mean, prove it." (Brian O'Keefe)

Critics are still skeptical and want long-term studies prior to a lengthy commitment. Much opposition to the process of hydraulic fracturing exists because of the harm it can cause to the environment as well as the dangers associated with jobs in fields related to fracking. During the process, a hole is drilled into the earth's surface and a layer of cement is put in to prevent the fracking fluid from contaminating aquifers, "bodies of saturated rock through which water can easily move." (Idaho Museum of Natural History) However, many people are skeptical as to how safe this is for the earth. The fractures made to release the natural gas from the rocks beneath the earth can allow the chemicals to seep into nearby groundwater. Studies show that methane concentrations in wells near fracking sites are 17 times higher than in those that are not near fracking sites. Over 1,000 cases of sensory, respiratory, and neurological damage from drinking contaminated groundwater have been reported. Jobs such as well-logging and hot oiling can lead to radiation exposure, unexpected release of pressure, explosions, fires, and other injuries, according to OSHA.

Questions and Variables

Are you willing to allow people (lawmakers, business associates, or investors) who will not be here 20 to 40 years from now to make decisions for your life and those of your future family? Are you willing to eat food that has been grown near a pipeline, and how would you know? These concerns are often not addressed when wells are drilled, which can be up to 18 times at one site. Companies will not put a label saying that their products were grown near what can be contaminated water, and many public officials will not think of what may happen in the future, only what is marketable and helpful to the economy now. Unbiased researchers who do not profit from or who are not required to show loyalty to an opinion, such as Larry Wackett, a biochemistry professor and a principal investigator for the project of cleaning fracking fluid believe, "We see ourselves at the University as not being on industry's side or the environmentalists' side. We're trying to solve a problem." (*Minnesota Daily*)

You, too, can make a difference in this major decision. Remember, we are talking about long-term decisions that will still have an impact 50 or more years from now. By contacting your local officials and joining local organizations, you can apply your voice to the decisions of today and get involved. You can learn new information about relevant topics by going online or to your local library and researching hydraulic fracturing. Topics that are relevant to fracking are often used in describing the process. Many environmentalists believe that safety controls for areas around the fracking wells should be implemented. Some fracking sites can contaminate pure water from aquifers that can be transported to metropolitan areas hundreds of miles away, such as from the Adirondack Mountains to New York City. So what do you think? Should we slow down the research and be more thorough in making the process safer? Are there ways we can input our voices into the data that moves this project forward? What platforms can we use to be heard—positively or negatively? Who are the leaders of tomorrow?

SINGNE BROWN, *Fantastic Animal*, Grade 12, Age 17. Moses Brown School, Providence, RI. Catherine VanLancker, *Educator*. 2014 Gold Medal

I'm a He, Not a Question Mark: The Trans Community Reflects on Issues of Identity, Sex, and Gender

JACKSON BROOK, Grade 11, Age 17. Palo Alto High School, Palo Alto, CA, Paul Kandell, *Educator*

Editor's Note: This story switches from using female pronouns to male pronouns for the main subject. The change is intentional.

Cameron was the girl with the unshaved legs and the close-cropped hair, the one who wore basketball shorts and played sports, who elicited the question: Is that a boy or a girl?

For much of her life, Cameron, now a Palo Alto High School student whose name has been changed for purposes of this story, struggled to answer this question, fending off unwelcome interrogation about her gender and her own feelings of ambivalence. At the heart of her conflict lay a division that arose between her inner self and her body. The majority of Cameron's life has been one long passage, a search for acceptance, not only from others but also from herself.

She was adopted at two and brought to Palo Alto, never knowing her biological parents. In her new home, she was raised by a loving family with two older brothers who gave her boyish hand-me-downs to wear, complementing the dark hair she kept trimmed short. Cameron liked the look, a remnant from her days in the orphanage. Besides, short hair was easier for her to manage.

"People knew me as a tomboy, and someone who just met me would usually call me a 'he,' but my friends would correct them," Cameron says. "I would always sigh to myself because I wanted to be known as a 'he.' I had this voice in the back of my head whispering 'he' whenever someone would call me a 'she.'"

Then came middle school, a turbulent period. It was in the forced intimacy of the girl's locker room that her path came to a crossroads.

"It was like my whole life came down this decision, where I had to decide whether I wanted to change in the girl's bathroom or not," Cameron says. "Was I a boy or a girl? I wasn't really sure, so I didn't change [for P.E.]."

Cameron always felt like her body was a nuisance, an incessant reminder that despite all her attempts to alter her appearance, she was still a girl, at least physically; wearing boy's clothes and binding her breasts could not change that. The very act of undressing in front of others would be exposing the feminine body that she sought desperately to ignore.

"It felt wrong," Cameron says. "It was a new school, and I didn't want people to see me and ask questions. I didn't want people to know [I was a girl]."

Cameron started sessions with her sixth-grade counselor but was hesitant to reveal her confusion about her gender identity until a month of board games and small talk had passed. Finally, she confessed that she felt uncomfortable changing in the girl's locker room. From then on, Cameron began meeting with an Adolescent Counseling Services counselor, who helped her deal with the complicated issues regarding her gender and to form a long-term plan of action. The meetings allowed Cameron to become aware of the underlying intuitions she had always felt about her gender and enabled her to ultimately embrace the masculine pronoun she always identified with: He.

He. His. Him. The words felt natural, authentic, and genuine, at last providing the tangible sense of recognition that had evaded Cameron for years. Now, having fully accepted his male identity, he faced the arduous process of reshaping the way others perceived his gender in light of his physical sex being female.

"I was finding out who I was, and people were finding out what my new identity was," says Cameron, who says that many of his peers did not comprehend the seriousness of his desire to change his physical appearance to match his gender.

"People would say, 'So you want to be a guy?' And they just don't get that I am. To me, it's like a slap in the face," Cameron says. "Sometimes I wish nobody knew. But people do know, so I just have to deal with it. I just wish people knew to call me a guy."

His parents thought it was a phase, a product of teenage angst and confusion, an attempt at self-expression that would fade away, like acne or hormones or any other unsavory aspect of adolescence.

Soon, their denial gave way to a belief that they were at fault.

"My parents thought they messed up and caused me to be transgender," Cameron says, referring to the short hair and boy's clothing. "But I think I was this way from the start."

Even though he has officially changed his gender, Cameron still feels in transition.

"It's hard to accept the fact that I'm transgender," Cameron says. "I feel like I shouldn't have to say it. I'll be thinking I'm a guy, and then something will happen and I'll remember that I'm transgender. It's like a reality check."

However, transgender students no longer have to worry about changing in the wrong locker room, thanks to Assembly Bill 1266, passed by the California legislature on August 12. The bill, designed to cut down on sex segregation, states among other matters that transgender students may "use facilities consistent with his or her gender identity, irrespective of the gender listed on the pupil's records."

This means that Cameron, who identifies as male, can now legally change clothes in the boy's locker room, use the boy's bathroom, and play on the boys' team in school sports. California is now the first state to provide transgender students legal rights to use sex-segregated facilities and participate in sex-segregated activities.

Furthermore, by acknowledging and supporting the basic rights of transgender students, AB 1266 ensures that schools will legitimize the premise presented by the trans community: that gender identity is more important than sex.

"We [transgender people] are not trying to be the opposite gender," Cameron says. "We really are like that. People don't get that I'm not trying to be a guy. I am a guy. That's what confuses them."

Along with the bill, there have been other current events suggesting an increasingly positive reception toward transgender students, most notably the attention surrounding Cassidy Lynn Campbell, a male-to-female senior who was crowned homecoming queen of Marina High School, in Huntington Beach, on September 20.

The passing of AB 1266 may signify how far society has come in accepting the LGBTQ community, yet there was a time when there was much less liberality regarding these issues.

Flashback to the 1980s

Jed Bell, a Palo Alto High School graduate of 1987 and female-to-male transgender, recalls that, in his four years of high school as a girl, there were no openly lesbian or gay students.

"I had two gay male friends, and they discussed it with no one," Bell says. "There was no telling how people would react." Bell didn't know he was trans at the time, just that he varied in his sexual orientation.

"All I knew was that when I fell in love, it was with girls," Bell says.

However, Bell, who was, in his own words, "a very butch" lesbian before he transitioned, considered himself to be innately male, even from a young age.

"I thought people were stupid because they were seeing me wrong and describing me wrong," Bell says. "They didn't understand the way I wanted to be thought of."

Like Cameron, he dealt with frequent interrogation about his gender from his peers.

"From my first day in school, kids were asking me, 'Are you a boy or a girl?' and it never stopped," Bell says. "There were some times where I was really depressed."

Yet because of society's lack of LGBTQ awareness, Bell had no way of knowing what he was going through, and so, for him, taking any sort of action was nearly impossible at the time.

"Back then, transgender, going female to male, was simply not on anyone's radar," Bell says. "It was not understood as a thing that existed. It wasn't until the '90s that somebody could realistically transition."

It was not until 1993, when Bell read *Stone Butch Blues* by Leslie Feinberg, a book portraying the struggles of a young lesbian, that he became aware of another person with whom he could identify. Several of Bell's lesbian friends recommended the book to him, telling him the book reminded them of him, almost as if they were reading his diary.

In the midst of perusing through *Stone Butch Blues*, Bell underwent a moment of profound clarity.

"When I saw the word transgender, I put the book down and felt a chill run down my spine, because I realized that's what I am," Bell says. "The whole time I was reading the book, I knew it was an experience that was changing my life. It was like this nebulous, cloudy, all-consuming weight had been lifted from my shoulders. I didn't know there was a word, or should be a word, for what I felt like. And I thought to myself, 'Now I know. This is a thing that has a name, and this is what I am.'"

Gender Identity

Jace Jamason, a Paly 2013 graduate and female-to-male transgender, starting thinking about his gender identity during Living Skills in 10th grade.

"It's funny, because everyone thinks of Living Skills as a joke class," Jamason says. "I had Ms. [Letitia] Burton, and there was this final project we did which caused me to think about it [my own gender identity]. Through online research for the project, I was introduced to the idea of being transgender."

"I was nurtured to be female, and as a result, I am very effeminate, yet I've always identified as male," Jamason says. "But I was never the monster-truck, macho kind of guy."

When Jamason came out to his parents, he noted mixed feelings in their reactions.

"While they were generally supportive, they wanted me to

be sure and to explore the thought," Jamason says. "My mom wants to be supportive, but she still doesn't understand the difference between my gender and my sex."

Burton, Jamason's Living Skills teacher at Paly, notes the way different individuals perceive their social identity.

The difference between sex and gender is essential to understanding the perspective of trans individuals: Whereas sex reflects itself through the body, gender lies beneath the surface.

"There's your social identity, which is how the world sees you, and it looks at issues of race, economic status, sexual orientation, whether you're a man or a woman, your gender identity, religion—these are all social identity pieces." Burton says. "Seeing how one relates to another, you look at which one you feel most connected to. Some people don't feel connected to their social identity at all, and other people feel like their social identity is a big part of their personal identity."

Jamason stresses the contrast between his internal and external selves.

"I've always been very separated from my body and withdrawn to my mind. It's like they're two different entities but very much a part of who I am," he says.

Jamason spoke at length with former Principal Phil Winston about how the school would deal with his gender, and as a result of the direct communication between Jamason and the administration, his gender never proved to be much of an issue.

"I had to use staff bathrooms though," Jamason says. "I would've liked to have been able to use the boy's bathroom, but I didn't feel that comfortable with myself yet."

Still, in other aspects of his life, Jamason's transition was not so uncomplicated.

"I identify as a gay male, but I've had experiences with both boys and girls," Jamason says. "I've had hook-ups, and one of them I wanted to turn into a relationship, but the other person didn't want to; they needed to grow into themselves more before they were ready."

On the other hand, Rae Marcum, who attended Palo Alto High School from 2009 to 2011 (through 10th grade), began transitioning from female to male during 11th grade, while in the middle of a relationship.

"My girlfriend doesn't care. She loves me for who I am as a person, not for my gender," says Marcum, who has been dating for over a year and a half.

Marcum knew he was attracted to girls while still in middle school, but it took him several years before he discerned that he was transgender.

"I finally started to understand what was going on, and I learned there were other options than from what you're assigned at birth," says Marcum, currently a freshman at Humboldt University.

Project Outlet

Many gender-nonconforming youth, also known as "queer and questioning," struggle to find a safe environment where they can try out new identities and explore their feelings.

One such setting can be found through a local organization, Project Outlet, on West El Camino Real at View Street in Mountain View. Outlet seeks to empower LGBTQ youth and, according to its website, "build safe and accepting communities through support, education and advocacy."

For Marcum, and other gender-questioning youth in Palo Alto, Outlet served as an inroad to the LGBTQ community. Marcum began trying out male pronouns during Outlet sessions.

"Outlet was a place where I could ask questions and be myself," Marcum says. "If I felt different each week, it would be fine, I wouldn't feel like I was being judged by others."

Anthony Ross, 41, has worked at Outlet since 1997 and acts as a facilitator for Outlet's weekly youth meetings. Ross stresses the importance of allowing kids to discover for themselves what gender they identify with and not pressuring them to conform with certain standards.

"If you just open the space for them and make it safe for them, they will just kind of explore," Ross says. "They'll let us know what feels best for them, and that can change as they grow . . . they feel more comfortable this way or that way."

Most children begin to differentiate between male and female around the ages of three and four, Ross says. Around this time, young children begin to express their nonconformity and variance in gender identity.

"Sometimes a male-bodied child will say, 'When do I get my vagina?' or 'When do I get to wear dresses?' A female-bodied child will start to say, 'When do I grow my penis?' They'll actually ask their parents these questions," Ross says. "It's because they're starting to realize that while they may feel one way, their bodies are different. It's an internal thing, what feels best for them, which they may need help trying to figure out."

Ross says that in many primary education settings, any attempt at merging gender boundaries, such as a boy who wants to wear a dress, can be met by parents and teachers with resistance or at the very least concern. However, Ross believes the key to dealing with nonconforming children is to give them room to develop their own unique identity.

Jamason suggests a similar approach to dealing with gender ambiguity.

"As humans we naturally like to put things in boxes, but people can be anywhere on the sexuality spectrum, either very gay or very lesbian or anywhere in between, and likewise, people shouldn't be gender-labeled," Jamason says.

Zander Davis, a history and sociology teacher at Palo Alto High School, echoes Jamason's statement.

"You look at school, look at what you get at home, what comes up in the media," Davis says. "There's an understanding of society based on the perception of what it means to be a man and what it means to be a woman. I think a key part of diversity that we're missing is mutual understanding and open conversation among people of all different classes and different types."

Davis believes that prejudices develop when people create generalities based on limited experiences to compensate for their lack of understanding regarding a specific group, such as the transgender community. The danger of labels, Davis says, is that it causes unfair assumptions to be made.

"When we live among them [people different than us] and have our kids play together and go to school together and have conversations together, we learn about them and then those prejudices fall apart and those labels fall apart," Davis says. "When we don't have diversity and we don't interact, then that's when labels acquire a lot of power."

Ross says that it can be difficult for young children or teenagers in the middle of the gender spectrum to identify with a specific group. To fill this vacuum, a new word, genderqueer, has emerged as an umbrella term to include gender-variant individuals in the LGBTQ community, without forcing them to choose a specific label.

"It [genderqueer] is a newer-generation word for gender-non-conforming or androgynous," Ross says. It's for people who are more in that middle spectrum of gender and not really pushing to those extremes of male or female. It's a term that a lot of youth use because it works for them more than transgender."

However, Marcum says that despite AB 1266, there is still room for improvement in schools to create a safer environment "Teachers should not separate students in any class by gender," Marcum says. "It happens a lot in P.E., but also in lots of other classes, where they'll say things like, 'Line up boy-girl, boy-girl' or 'Boys on this side of the room, girls on that side.' It's very uncomfortable for someone who is transgender but not out."

However, regardless of their surrounding environment, Marcum emphasizes the need for youth (or adults) questioning their gender to stay in touch with their emotions and not inhibit themselves because of perceived societal constraints.

"Let yourself question, let yourself feel whatever you're feeling, don't box yourself in," Marcum says. "Find resources and people to talk to and have conversations with them. You are the most important person, you are around yourself every day, and so if you're not happy with yourself, you're not going to be happy with anything."

Of Misanthropy

PHILIP ANASTASSIOU, Grade 12, Age 17. Bergen Academies, Hackensack, NJ, Rebecca Strum, *Educator*

To my mother.

CHARACTERS
THE MATERNAL CHORUS—a Greek chorus of mothers
THE GIRL—a teenage girl
THE BOY—a teenage boy

SETTING
A graveyard

A NOTE ON PUNCTUATION
A slash ("/") in the midst of a line indicates when the other actor should begin speaking their next line, so that both actors are simultaneously speaking.

"If the water were clear enough, If the water were still, but the water is not clear, the water is not still."
—Stanley Kunitz

1. (Ominous lights rise on a graveyard. It looks peculiar. The tombstones are noticeably small and labeled only with numbers anywhere from the hundreds to the millions. Heaps

of trash made of current technology (flat-screen TVs, electric ovens, fancy dishwashers, etc.) are stacked as though to act as a barrier to the outside. The foliage has been left ungroomed for what could be years, and now vines consume an occasional entire tombstone.

The sound of a deep, thick rumble is heard, followed by the gentle weeping of a newborn baby. It continues, its volume rising and falling like inconstant waves, as THE MATERNAL CHORUS enters.

They are women of grit and shit, donned in distressed rags made to appear as makeshift armor. They wear black ski masks that cover their faces, except their eyes and mouth. On their bodies: grenades, machine guns, knives. Some pregnant, others not. More important, however, they inhabit the apparent dichotomy that they are as barbaric as they are beautiful. They enter cautiously, weapons prepared to be drawn at the slightest unusual sound, but with a certain conviction.

This is their land. These graves are of their dead. You are not welcome here.)

THE MATERNAL CHORUS #1: God is dead.

THE MATERNAL CHORUS #2: And yet, somehow, we are alive.

THE MATERNAL CHORUS #3: What difference does it make, though?

THE MATERNAL CHORUS #4: Here, there is no method to distinguish one from the other.

#2: They are one and the selfsame thing.

#1: One comes, one goes.

#3: One breathes, one doesn't.

#4: But what are we to do about it?

#1: Such is life, after all.

#2: And life is brief.

#3: It is hard, and what's more, it ends.

#4: What a shitty sort of contact this is.

#1: But we do not fight it, we mothers.

#4: No, no, we abide to this great agreement because we are reasonable people who care for their children.

#2: We do what we must.

#3: And though we aren't the handsomest of those you may stumble upon in these parts, we are very charming.

#4: And if you think otherwise, we have these to make up for it.

[They make their weapons too visible for comfort and grin in unison.]

#3: In any case, be sure to know you are not welcome here.

#2: This is not a place for the faint of heart.

#1: The stench alone is enough to dissuade otherwise blood-thirsty buzzards from dining here.

#4: This is our land.

#2: These graves are of our dead.

#1: All those six feet under were but seconds old before they died.

#3: From the womb of their mother to the womb of this soil,

they all have made the transition . . . for the most part . . . with elegance.

#2: But do not mistake these numbers for people.

#1: These tombstones signify nothing.

#4: They hadn't even the chance to be honored with a name before they died.

#3: So these numbers will have to do in the meantime, absolving what few sins can be made in such briefness.

#2: But do we mourn? Hardly.

#3: What an awful notion, you must think.

#4: Mothers who do not mourn for their dead children?

#1: What monsters, what cruelty.

#4: No, no. You hardly understand.

#2: You see, we do it ourselves.

#3: Just as they are brought into this world at our own expense, we end them.

#1: Do not stare at us with these looks of disgust.

#4: Smile . . .
[THE MATERNAL CHORUS smiles in unison.]
. . . as we do.

#2: We smile because we know what we do comes from the deepest well of love reserved only for mothers and their children.

#3: Look at what little belongs to us.

#1: This makeshift armor?

#4: This dirt?

#1: These rags?

#2: Such poverty is enough for us to bear alone.

#3: This unending hunger makes you think profoundly bad thoughts.

#2: It makes you vengeful.

#4: It makes you hate.

#1: Deep hatred as thick as blood.

#3: This unquenchable thirst makes you wish you had died before you were even given the chance to learn your own name.

#1: We all wish this.

#3: No, no.

#4: What sort of mothers are we to force these burdens upon our very own?

#3: The ones who we love the most in this world?

#2: How could we allow them to be polluted when they are so safe just as they are when they are born?

#4: How could we?

#1: So, it has been decided upon.

#4: We have all agreed.

#3: It is not from malice, but from affection.

#1: As soon as they arrive, they must depart.

#2: We do not cry.

#3: We do what we must.

#2: We will not cry.

#4: Most of them resign to their fate with grace and simplicity.

#3: Of course, they may protest for a moment, but inevitably must give in one way or another.

#2: Dirt fills the cavities of their bodies . . .

#4: Their nostrils, their ears, their gaping mouths . . .

#1: Their shrills are quieted to a silence reserved only for the defeated . . .

#2: Such a pure silence is unheard of to most . . .

#3: But it is there without a doubt . . .

#1: We have the great privilege of hearing it . . .

#4: And we listen . . .

#2: We listen deeply . . .

[They close their eyes and we listen to the purest of all silences. A heavy moment and then they resume.]

#3: We watch as peace settles on their young faces . . . and then they are no more.

#4: After all, no one is ever as well-regarded as the moment immediately after they die.

#1: Those who have forgotten you as they aged toward expiration suddenly remember.

#3: They recall you.

#2: They contemplate you.

#4: Granted, their thoughts are not always good ones, but they are candid nonetheless.

#1: But even so, not every creature of our making can be perfect.

#3: Some refuse it.

#2: No matter how hard we try.

#4: Some deny it.

#1: We must find another way to deal with them.

#3: These are the ones who do not cooperate.

[The sound of a vexed, screeching baby can be made out. It progressively intensifies to an unbearable point and serves as underscoring for the following lapse.]

#4: They cry at first, like all others, in the absence of obvious affection.

#1: But instead, their cries do not end.

#2: Even after they are birthed directly into these graves, they are not pleased.

#3: Still, the hole is filled and we move on with our lives.

#1: But if you press your ear to the ground, you can still hear them screaming.

#2: From feet below, under pounds of packed dirt, you can still hear their weeping.

#4: It is such a simple, simple sound.

#2: And yet, it is made of all human hatred and suffering.

#4: A graveyard of the potential for those who refused to give in.

#1: They haunt you for hours, and even when it ends, it rings in our head for years afterward.

#3: But we do not let them out.

#2: We do not dig them out.

#1: We cannot break our pact.

#4: We will not let them suffer!
[One of them shoots their gun into the sky. It is a climax. The sound of the baby screeching in pain suddenly stops. We hear the beautiful, pure silence they spoke of earlier.]

To read this play in its entirety, visit **www.artandwriting. org/galleries**

The Goldsmith

AYLA JEDDY, Grade 7, Age 13. The Dalton School, New York, NY,
Inanna Donnelley, *Educator*

Circa 2600-2400 B.C.E.

It was hot
I'll tell you that.

There were tools everywhere,
hammers, and materials.

But mostly
I remember the fire.

The terrible cruel fire
that melted me to liquid.

The warm beautiful fire
that allowed me to be completed.

And the same dancing orange flames
that then created my twin.

*"The Goldsmith" is one of several poems that follow the story
of an ancient Mesopotamian statue called "Ram Caught in a
Thicket" throughout some of the stages in its history.*

Insomnia

STEPHANIE GUO, Grade 12, Age 17. Canyon Crest Academy,
San Diego, CA. Lisa Caston and Jennie Chufo, *Educators*

is the great unifier. at times it deserts us in the desert, leaving us to wander from oasis to oasis with creaking, half-lidded eyes. at other times, we find ourselves unable—unwilling, even—to distinguish dreams from reality. our dreams taste like cotton candy, overwhelmingly soft and sweet and fleeting. we want to brush our teeth four times a day—once in the morning, once at night, once in the dream-morning, and once at dream-night. we possess two subscriptions of the same newspaper, two identical best friends with the same unutterable penchant for brussel sprouts, two cats with the same tortoiseshell pattern dappled across the tutting tips of their tails. we possess two universes, and yet the great unifier only allows to become well-versed in one—

so we cut and snip. we decide on a mistress and we decide on a wife. we trim and trip. we leave the mistress on a ship bound for the bottom of the sea and are initiated into the cult of cubicle. occasionally a message in a bottle washes up on the beach. themermaidshaveadoptedme, the mistress explains. andloveis—we give the bottle to the wife and mull things over with the help of Anheuser-Busch, almost convincing ourselves that we could live in just this one universe forever, because putting our hands up in the middle of the road is simpler, isn't it?

Hurricane Kaoru

LATROY ROBINSON, Grade 12, Age 17. Oak Park & River Forest High
School, Oak Park, IL, Peter Kahn, *Educator*

Whenever a hurricane arises
my mother watches wide-eyed.
She always counts down the days
it takes for the hurricane to breach shore.
Her lips pearl back, baring a smile
She thinks hurricanes are the strongest thing out there.
Everyone bows to them as they strut down the street.
They can swing their hips into buildings and no one will
    punish them.
She loves that Andrew can shift cities,
that Sandy can drop towers off her shoulder,
that Rita can swing a town with her windy whips.
She is enthralled by the destructive blessing
left behind, thinks it's an art sweeter than poetry.

My father doesn't want me to go to New Orleans for college.
He knows my mother would be too eager to visit.
He said he took her there once, and she loved it too much.
She was so caught in the aftermath, the broken blessed
    buildings.
My father says she became too wild there,
that she'd whirl from bar to bar,
finishing only half of a conversation,
yelling at randoms on the street,
dancing on destroyed land,
asking everyone when they thought She would come back.
The real reason why my mother loves it down there.

She wishes she could meet Mother Katrina,
learn how to crescent a city in a drunken rage,
learn how to rip homes from men to make them bow.

I think my mother wants to become a storm-headed woman.
To bless and not get punished,
to have everyone know that she isn't someone you can
    shoo away.
I'm scared that this will lead her down a blood drunken path,
turn her into a natural-made disaster.
The kind that curses,
the kind that makes America not want to send relief,
the kind that we don't want to name.

Ordinary Travel

MICHAEL SHORRIS, Grade 11, Age 16. Hunter College High School, New York, NY, Kip Zegers, *Educator*

'I seek a tourniquet for my mind'
says a man on the J train.
I like his syntax and wonder if I could fashion my own version
of such a device.
But his profusely bleeding left calf makes a more compelling
case for aid,
so some police wrap him up and take him away.
I think I'll miss him.

He leaves a small pool of red that turns a gruesome brown on
the speckled floor;
'shit on the robin's egg' announces a man with a grey do-rag
and a *Brooklyn* hat.
I seek his eloquence in my own writing.
It oozes from one side of the car to the other as we rock on the
    Marcy el.
I hear a woman scream Fuck me? No, fuck *you*! into a small
    plastic phone;
I'm more taken aback by her cellular service in the subway
than her language.

A drop into the tunnel
while sweet Southern tones glide out of three middle-aged
    black men.
They entertain with eccentric clothes and eccentric
    expressions,
performing caricatures of men I know they are not.
They have too much pride for this shabby occupation, and for
    that I admire them more.

They sing, and soul resonates against plastic seats and steel
   expressions,
the high treble of jangling change balancing warm baritone
voices.

I think this is urban peace.

Tranquility was broken
as a higher being spoke to me.
The man was nearly a foot taller than I was,
balding head delicately tucked beneath the air-conditioning.
His dry mouth spat prophetic words about a savior I didn't
   know very well
though vaguely hoped to meet.

Feeling guilty for lack of piety,
I offered a crumpled bill in an outstretched hand to one of
the soul men;
thought I'd created my own tourniquet out of charity,
wondered if I'd bought my way into heaven.
[Crushed when I remembered I wasn't religious,
I considered taking back my donation.]

Maybe I was unhinged,
but it was then that it hit on a Broad Street-bound J train.
Charity wouldn't buy redemption,
nor would it patch this slowly hemorrhaging mind.
My tourniquet would need more than white guilt and spare
   change.
Until I'd made it, I'd never find my peace
and so I quietly hoped for some officers to take me away, too.

Racism in America

DARRELL HERBERT, Grade 12, Age 17. High School for Health Professions & Human Services, New York, NY, Sebastian Natera, *Educator*

Love me
The fake rappers got choppers
The fake actors got Oscars
The government aren't mobsters
The Illuminati impostors
Cruel world, that's all I ever really heard
And life is Hell so I always listen to God's words
Don't love them girls
They just birds
Though love seems to be last when it comes first
Haters keep hating me because it's dead in the hearse
My heart is broke because my real life and my love life
really hurts
And I always try to set a good example
And God has given me so many problems I can't handle
Pray forgiveness
All my thoughts are written on a hit list
And everything I've killed for just became a witness
And who sell
And they fell when they went to jail
But our corrupt society wants us all to fail
Jesus help
Praying to you later
Asking God for favors
And my strive to success will help me overcome all the haters

You'll never feel my pain
Blood in deceivers

My depression has grievance
Assassinated our leaders
Who's going to lead the people
Lying and stealing
What is this feeling
I hate feeling lonely because it was it
Forgive all the sins I commit
The world need to change
This is embarrassing it
And Martin had a dream but he was killed before he realized it
I was a wild guy
Dying in moments like this
Confidential secrets are the reason the world is how it is
We in a city where the cops just shoot and hit
Tell me who was I
And I'll admit I've felt alone for most of my pathetic life
Rapping on a track
Using violence won't solve crap
In a world where the girls get mistreated or slapped
Fathers start being a man
Sons stop selling crack
And they say love is like a war
So why these girls don't love me back
Now the student is the master
Now the underdog's a grad
Now the jobs that we do help us have what we have

You'll never feel my pain
You'll never feel my pain
You'll never understand if you never known

The Walrus

ROBERT ELLIOTT WYATT, Grade 8, Age 14. Logan School, Denver, CO,
Max Maclay, *Educator*

There he was, a viperous grin on his face,
Standing right outside this preposterous place.
Trampling over the well-cared-for lawn,
With an exuberant gluttony that was far from withdrawn.

He had two boney tusks stretching down past his throat,
And he sweated black liquid down onto his coat.
His jagged gray mustache stuck horizontally away,
From his bulbous red nose, and his disoriented gaze.

He waved up at me, in my balcony seat,
To go play chess or checkers in the warm summer heat.
And that's how I spent my long afternoons,
Playing games with a walrus, and whistling tunes.

Rita Hayworth, Actress, 1947

EMILY MACK, Grade 10, Age 16. Northside College Preparatory
High School, Chicago, IL, Nora Flanagan, *Educator*

"You are my life—my very life."
—Orson Welles in a letter to Rita Hayworth

James Hill had a vicious tongue and he loved it
when I cried. He used to make me cry in the bedroom
or while he held my hand, he used to make me cry
at dinner parties, he got my face into my elbow,
and the tears on white tablecloth once made Charles Heston
so uncomfortable, he left apologetically.
After I met Orson, I filed for divorce on grounds of cruelty.
Orson saved me.
He sent me love letters that said,
Dearest Angel Girl,
and I hid them in my makeup case and I married him
in a blouse at City Hall and an hour later we returned
to the studio for work. Before I danced on-screen,
I had black hair and a widow's peak,
before they de-Latinized me,
and when I told him this, he chuckled dark,
said he once directed Julius Caesar, said he liked the sheen
of a real knife on stage and during rehearsal he accidentally
stabbed a man named Joseph Holland, and then I told him
    I was pregnant.
The next morning, I got two love notes instead of one.
When I felt her kick, I sent a prayer she would be like him,
recognized and prodigal, artistic and angry,

I prayed she would make movies,
not dance in them.
My career grew with my stomach, and continued
even after Rebecca's birth—people wanted Rita Hayworth
while Orson was shut out of Hollywood,
a self-exiled mastermind within himself,
he hid beneath sweat and white shirts that got looser each
year.
He screamed a lot and I let my daughter watch me drink.
No one was ever home.
Then I did *The Lady of Shanghai* for him
and the hair that I sold my soul for, those auburn locks
fell softly to the floor the first day of shooting. He stole the
    color
too, a distasteful platinum blonde. Behind the camera,
he grinned. In my role, I could not move, could not
dance the way everyone loved,
the way I loved
and *The Lady of Shanghai* flopped.
I filed for divorce that year,
and I told the press, "I can't take
his genius anymore," those were my grounds.

A Lesson in
Accepting Departure

ORIANA TANG, Grade 11, Age 16. Livingston High School,
Livingston, NJ, Fredrica Glucksman, *Educator*

1.
Third grade down Chinatown: the rancid
wretch of the open-air market—butchers
wielding silver knives, slitting fish with a twirl of blades.
Their scales gleam in late-afternoon sun, heat
shimmering off the sidewalks like a body through water.
Grandpa holds tight my hand, his other
gripping a basket. We weave the crowds. Amid the dicing
of fish heads is the murmur of feet and babble, the
shouts of street vendors. Vegetables—peppers, tomatoes—
their skin stretched so tight you can feel the way they would
snap between your teeth, taste the crisp of the flesh.
Grandpa drags me past the fish. I see a splatter of red
on the wooden cutting board, a limp body slid
into a plastic bag in the hand of a customer—
and then we are gone, past them.

2.
My first pets—from Grandpa, from the market. An old man
sitting on a fold-out chair in front of a grocery, a glossed cane
hooked by his side. Between his feet, a yellow basin
of sink water and goldfish, painted blurs of black-orange-
silver streaking like headlights in the dark. Sunlight
rippling through, glancing off their sleek bodies in shafts.
At Grandpa's direction the man, bald, shriveled,

lowers a plastic bag into the basin with a shaking hand
peppered with sunspots. Through his fingers the fish swim
    inside.
When he hands me the bag, he grins wordlessly, his mouth
full of broken.

3.
Later this is what I will remember. Not the way they died,
years later in a big glass tank, one by one,
their relentless graceful streaking
stopped as they floated up through the water
to touch air at last, or the dead splash they made
when we dropped each body into the toilet
to be flushed away,
but the way they left the old man's basin,
its smooth plastic walls, its safeties, the dirty water
they called home—a slip past thick hands, slick. Disappearing
somewhere new. The way the old man sat there,
still smiling, his fish leaving in the arms
of a girl clinging to her grandfather,
their shadows stretching long on the dusty streets.
You let them go.

Oil

CAMILA SANMIGUEL, Grade 8, Age 13. United Day School,
Laredo, TX, Stacy Burton, *Educator*

Why is it that
I am the one leper in the empire
who is known for
nothing
except permanent immaturity and ignorance,
translucent cotton stuffing and infant snails
bubbling in a round flannel belly
?
Why does no one realize
that I have the smarmy butterfly's crimson eyes
and I can see the black deltas in their brains
hear the blood constantly simmering on low in their eyeholes
and taste the bitter feces threatening to tumble from their lips
every time they smirk and blow
lumpy lipstick bubbles, kiss
acrid stubble concealing fangs
?
Why don't they ever perceive anything
other than yellow larded tubs
and defective grins, and
stupid flyaway halos on mismatched
angels—the ones that stick out
like a lonely sock?
no, more like a walloping
heart
amongst millions of empty corpses.

You pretend to know and talk and laugh
about meaningless
bullshit
.

I cannot assimilate
how I am barred from destroying
a heartspace inflated with deleterious dioxide.
reduce it to stinging splinters
and burnt, shimmering shards
reflecting the smoke that warbles beneath
because of the moles curled in the cobwebbed spinal crevices
.

And it brings rough, leaden tears to my eyes
to think of these people
who swallow lies;
these people who have contaminated me.
A vicious murk incessantly trickles through my dry veins,
leaving me
with an emptying love
I cannot extricate or excrete;
a yearning and sorrow for them—the ones that ignorantly dwell
in my hatred
.

Yet, I will not have the sour faith
to ever exorcise the growing parasite that is
sucking on the dank lining of my thorax
and it is distorting me, making me sweat
the painful tears of Delilah
that are ancient yet fresh;
like He with poison breath blew coarse glass from silverwet
crystals
tomorrow.

Dolbear's Law

NOA GUR-ARIE, Grade 11, Age 16. Bethesda-Chevy Chase High School, Bethesda, MD, Sarah Mahoney, *Educator*

To love as a cricket does:
to occupy an ear, a blade
of grass, to see with eyes like
cut stones,
to behold the miraculous
pebbles sitting unprecious,
a hundredfold, a millionfold,
to sing for dirt, to bring cut-up
wings together in hymn and count
time as the sky goes cold, tempo
for temperature, louder even than the
cone-headed katydids, to listen
closely with the crook of a knee for
a harmony of veins, to sing
to be heard by everything, earth and
air and sky and you, muscles
thrumming with the atmosphere,
symphony for the soil.

Em

SOPHIA DIGGS-GALLIGAN, Grade 8, Age 13. Deal Middle School,
Washington, D.C., Elizabeth Gutting, *Educator*

Metal chains that are paper thin,
like a string, and you forget that they are binding you,
that you bound yourself.

I found you, crouched,
foetal,
in a shopfront window,
Hiding behind the racks of men's pants
and leather belts,
crying softly for the patron saint
of all the children
who got lost in
department stores
—and never came back.

The windows were bound with
copper alloy,
it stank of denial
and hidden perfection.

You donate in small denominations.

You stepped away from
the eyes and the crush of crowd
and people forcing their everything on you.

stark blindness.
Into the cold and the boxwood and the snow
the sharpness of winter perfuming the air

stabbing you at the intake,
like
all the deafening silence.

no response, it would never come.
lost in a sea, a vale of feigned tears
—you didn't care.
and that is what hurt the most.

you always
used the same PA announcement.

crackling and sputtering in robotic voices,
in grocery stores, over television.

Everyone heard them, but he.

Oh, really?

you never
waited to hear the response.

Static washed over his
life and his hiding place.

Come, static and slanted sunlight.
Come and wash over me.

How Black Curls
Were Invented

JULIA TOMPKINS, Grade 12, Age 18. Saint Ann's School,
Brooklyn Heights, NY, Martin Skoble, *Educator*

Even though my dad wasn't one for woodpeckers
or elastic waistbands,
he still followed his brothers
to church each Sunday.

After school he'd stand by the altar being good, not like I am
    good at bed-making
but because he knew how
to believe in God.

My mother was a lot of split in two, with a dad
that did summers and sent her off to college, and
a mom who did the seventies like it was her
job.

Neither knew much about making things last, but
my dad built summertime houses in Cape May
that have made it through many a winter, in the city
where he did long hair and surfing and took out girls
in powder blue, they'd ask him his birthday and where
he learned to laugh like that.

My mother did dinners
alone and had hair that could be the spring in your step
if you wanted it to. By the time she got to college she
did all black and French Conversation and clove cigarettes,
even followed a boyfriend to Europe, but came home

alone because unlike her daughter my mother knows
the right way to say goodbye.

My father tried to be as much of a not-Jersey boy as he
could but it was his tan forearms that caught my mother's
attention, so much that she bought a stereo and had a
party, even started a study group so she could get
this boy into her life, so they could lie on a single
bed and listen to the Talking Heads and believe that
youth is indelible, that they, and I, and we would never
lose the look of happy people, and that would tie us
all together,

even though my dad smiles upside-down and
my mom cried when we couldn't buy the right cake for
my sister's birthday, and I've never learned how to fill
up space with silence, but we've all got blue eyes and
corrective lenses and maybe that will be enough.

This Is a Poem for Airing Dirty Laundry

MICHAL LEIBOWITZ, Grade 12, Age 17. Yeshiva University
High School, Hollis, NY, Audi Hecht, *Educator*

This is a poem for airing dirty laundry,
because the washing machine is broken and
these stains have a way of spreading

We have decades of contempt to scrub out of these sheets,
years of matzo crumbs versus wine stains versus bacon grease
   versus "kosher style"
and the only way to get the stink out is the gray steel wool
my mother uses to scrub the couscous pot,
peeling layers of noodle skin back from the black gaping walls
like flesh from a chicken

Chassidic and
Reform and
Modern Orthodox and
Reconstructionist
(which my father likes to say isn't really Judaism at all)

We toss e-mails and letters and protests back and forth
like a hot potato no one wants.
There are Jews who stand by the side of Fifth Avenue
with posters and signs and uglyyellingthreateningscreams
saying Zionism is a dirty word and those who support it
a dirty people

We have been instilled from birth with a magical
   Jew-detector,

allowing us to categorize religiosity by the cloth covering a
body:
Long bouncing sideburns and a fox fur *streimal* =
religious extremist
Skirts skimming knees and suits on the Sabbath = delusional,
because everyone knows it's impossible to be truly religious
and
modern at once
Pants on girls and sleeveless shirts and big purple skull caps
only ever worn for that cousin's bar mitzvah = sacrilegious
And then there are those Jews with
foreskins intact and strapless bikinis and Christmas trees in
December who we don't really have a name for because
they are so far gone.

Somehow the only things we all seem to agree on
is that anyone less religious is a heretic, and everyone more
is a
fanatic, and we
(whoever we may be)
are the only ones with our heads screwed on straight.

We have split ourselves across scriptural lines
based on minute discrepancies turned chasms, miles wide,
and now we are waiting with the air of a crowd at the
    coliseum—itching to see which of our brothers will be
swallowed by the earth.

Lost in Death Valley

RYAN JIMENEZ JENKINS, Grade 7, Age 12. Capistrano Valley
Christian Schools, San Juan, Capistrano, CA, Clarissa Ngo, *Educator*

We had a bowl of grapes and half a bottle of water
The day we got lost in Death Valley
On the day of the Big Fire
Just four kids and one mom in a broken-down Escalade with
a flat tire
And no salvation in sight

The white sand hills were as barren as our hopes
They stared at us with unseeing eyes
Like the ancient Great Pyramids of Giza
Where the dead sleep inside

As my mom passed out one red grape each
I savored that one grape for an hour
Lolling it about my tongue
To suck its sweet juices

I buried myself in my Seek-and-Find book
Trying to find the stop sign and the bear
So I wouldn't hear my mom crying

And then there was silence
Even the dust tasted like sadness
As a lone tumbleweed bumped and rolled past our truck
Right out of Death Valley
I wanted to hop on and follow it to freedom

But then we saw it
An old blue car in the distance
We ran-trudged-stumbled in a fog of dust

Hoping for something, anything that was inside
But it was just an empty broken-down old blue car
With nobody in it

We put a note on the windshield
Hoping that someone would return to collect their car
And then we trudged back
Held hands and prayed

Seconds later, a dust plume rolled over the mountain
Our hearts knocked against our ribs in terror
"The fire is coming!" we cried, squeezing each other's hands
A big red tow truck emerged from the plume
And we burst out of the truck, singing and waving our hands
Under the scorching rainbow-sherbet sky

MARGARET ZACKERY, *Refuge*, Grade 9, Age 14. Lakeridge High School, Lake Oswego, OR. Shannon McBride, *Educator*. 2014 Gold Medal

Cheeseburgers

ALEXANDER ZHANG, Grade 12, Age 17. Little Rock Central High School, Little Rock, AR, Scott Hairston, *Educator*

A geography teacher once told me
that ninety percent of Asian-Americans
are lactose intolerant.

Somewhere between the cookbooks of tradition
and Paula Deen recipes,
we have forgotten our dietary handicap.

My father plops two chunks of beef on the plate but first
smells the sweet sesame seeds on the buns—
this is a delicacy he remembers as home.

Below, two square lily pads yellower than my palms,
they settle above the lumps like
landing zones for helicopters of hunger.

The dairy blonde arms tuck below the patty
as if hugging the country while
sandwiched between oceans of wheat.

"Cheddar?"
"American."

A crooked smile before I bite.
I think: nothing could compare
to this manufactured 'Merica.

But irony is the drive-thru of McDonald's,
that forbidden city where I would shout,
"number three, please" above bickering
Mandarin from the passenger seat.

When I turned sixteen,
I asked for a Mustang in red, as if
Mustang or red would make ordering a Big Mac simpler.

The first time I drove alone with cheeseburger bits
dangling from my lips,
the only fear I felt was
being another Asian driver.

As I pulled away with Coca-Cola in hand,
the rear-view mirror asked
if I'd like to supersize the fries.

I glanced at the car behind and saw that
here is the scrawny me and there is the All-American,
I wish I were, a pilot who landed jet planes of
calories on outstretched tongue,
or a dining car conductor ripping through
my transcontinental railroad.

I am guzzling eighteen miles a gallon,
but I am fed like an import.

This vehicle is more cattle than pony,
more stutter than strut,
with an empty milk tank that
no one can quench.

God's Fury (a haibun)

VIVIANA PRADO-NUÑEZ, Grade 10, Age 15. George Washington Carver Center for Arts and Technology, Towson, MD, Suzanne Supplee, *Educator*

Cement blocks domino up the side of a gray Styrofoam mountain as flashing cameras trudge into slanting railroad cars. They hold on to metal bars with pudgy sausage fingers and wait to begin their ride up Montserrat.

> Shorts and Barbie legs,
> Eyes drifting and mouths giggling,
> Flies buzzing in skulls.

"I can't figure out her race."
They don't know me, yet still, their voices echo through the trees where animals no longer live. The fire had burned, licking with sandpaper tongues, singeing off fur—God's fury on a holy mountain.
"What's up wth her hairband? It's weird."
Where is God's fury? It shall come and leave decimated tree limbs for miles.
"Guys, I think she's looking at us."

Puckered lips, death stare,
and beasts move up the mountain—
they are rumbling.

Toes braced against sloping gravel lined with Van Gogh trees, I call my mom to come look at the view—the mountains are giant, mossy shark teeth tearing into the sky. We are alone and the world is my valley. This is God's fury.

Watching Little Boys Become Monsters (or Maybe They Always Were)

AVA GOGA, Grade 10, Age 15. Robert Mc Queen High School, Reno, NV,
Amie Newberry, *Educator*

At five and a half,
he is ruler of a kindergarten kingdom
A monkey-bar maniac
asphalt-skinned knee from all the times
he'd tripped trying to catch me.

At six,
he is five months older than me
but I am miles taller
He is all blonde hair and green eyes
and blue tongued from the
candy hearts he'd been breaking between his teeth.

At eight,
he is the face I wake up to most mornings
single night sleepovers stretch to a week
He wonders what it feels like to kiss
and so do I
We try it once and pull away giggling.

At eleven,
he is a summertime soldier
capturing insects and snakes
and other things that cannot defend themselves

We kiss again and he is all teeth
He says that's how they do it on tv.

At thirteen,
he is voice cracking bad haircut phase
first concert and we sneak away
to watch the big kids smoke weed
Afterwards he says he'll make it up to me
and teaches me to fish the next day.

At fifteen,
he is all Doberman Pinscher smiled
sleek-bodied football player
Catholic high school bad boy
I am all confused sexuality
but he knows exactly what he wants.

Seventeen,
He is finally taller than me
He is classroom king at his own convenience
knows what alcohol tastes like
carries condoms in his wallet but they are never old
He does not hope to "get lucky"
He has other ways
of getting what he wants.

Cartography

ALANA SPENDLEY, Grade 12, Age 17. Academy of the Holy Angels,
Demarest, NJ, Nancy Schneberger, *Educator*

I find that I
Am two things:
A poem and a body, with
Limbs of letters and bright
Movements in the syntax.
This heart beats all upon
The curvature of Earth;
I dig out verses
Like an archaeologist,
Excavating skulls to find
Bones like my own.
But more often, words
Peek out from the bottom
Of a dresser drawer, quaintly
Seeking to be seen.
I pluck stanzas from the places
Where your hair anoints
The skin of your neck
And shadows bless its pale craters.
The blind man on the
Subway paints a thousand
Strokes for me when he brushes
My shoulder on a subway.
There is poetry in the mother
Raising four children on
Holy water and communion wafers.

There is poetry in the boy
Who keeps himself hidden in
Sound waves, thick songs perforating
The surface of the empty
Silence that settles around
Like a tent when he was scared
To hear the sound of the woods—
Bones shattering.
There is poetry in
All you weary mothers, and you
Fathers far away, big-handed
With portal palms
Or clenched fists.
There is poetry in exploring every
Bend and break, every
Sloping hill and caving
Canyon beneath your
Birthmarks like points
On a globe.
All bodies hold poets because
We are apprentices of our own cartography;
Mapless, we walk among the
Poems we find.

Winter

C. SOPHIA GEORGE, Grade 7, Age 12. Park Tudor School,
Indianapolis, IN, Elizabeth Odmark, *Educator*

In silence
starry oceans sweep through the streets
gather, die, reform
crystals desperately cling to gutters
velvet blankets cover the sleeping grass

candles wink through a closed window
tentative feet
touch down to the cold
soundlessly

a figure stumbles onto the blank canvas
intricately weaving a path of footprints
silence encloses
and a million frozen stars
softly land on the ground

They Sold Them Down the River for a Song

GEORGE COUNTS, Grade 12, Age 17. Charleston County School of the Arts, North Charleston, SC, Francis Hammes, *Educator*

This story belongs to Granddaddy,
though he tells it with reluctance
and sour mash bobbing in
his coffee mug.
He leans his right arm slick against
the kitchen's marble counter-top,
his left hand embedded in the fabric
of his pocket.
And he begins slow and hot,
tongue-tied to each phrase,
chewing the sediment of his youth—
the topsoil and forehead sweat,
iron hoes and cotton—
each word pulled taut
like the strings of a steel guitar.

The scene set:
blackened faces strained against a windowpane.
Children.
Their heavy overall cuffs wet with blood
and cotton brambles,
toes bent and calloused,
straw hats and T-shirts shield them from the sun,
the vast earth immobile beneath their feet.
My granddaddy and his five brothers

watched as electricity trickled into Hahn's Village,
a shriveled crop-lien on Carolina's western border.
There were blue star petals and box elders,
Confederate banners,
sweet as cherry juices running down his lips.
Their shack wedged deep in a ramshackle, two-bucket,
farming town, scarred by rust and Governor Johnston's
runny gaze.

II.
A single bulb,
white as lye soap,
pregnant with light,
cleansing.
The family's Bible underneath,
its spine fired leather
its pages yellowing teeth.
A single bulb;
swinging back and forth,
a manacle in the country wind,
which whistled lovely and fine
that summer
in 1938,
its wind colored with the snap
of nooses against bark.
And my granddaddy,
the bravest son,
the tin soldier as
gaunt as one of Thurmond's bony fingers,
puffed out his chest and wandered
into the cabin
as the company-man rigged the wire

through the walls.
And he approached the bulb
in a sort of stone-faced trance of
fear and wonder.

III.
And I wonder now,
sitting at my writing desk,
far removed from those killing fields,
by a good half-century,
if he reached out and cupped each bright ray,
if he let the light flood his body,
envelop the synapses aflutter in his skull,
held together the longing tucked within his ribcage
(that blue thing his mother called a soul).
I wonder if he touched the bulb
and felt its blanket-warmth,
wonder if he shielded himself from the
faults and cracks that linger in the bones of
all Black southerners.
Those shadows
with funny names
like Plessey
and Till
and Vesey
and Norma Jean,
the girl my granddaddy courted
in the summer of '44,
the girl he found stamped into the earth
one day,
face-down,
sweat and blood pooling

and undulating like the muck
of the Mississippi,
a girl made a rag-doll by the Reconstructed South
and its tendrils,
all fire and torn lace,
tattered at the seams
like the old coat
Joseph was sold for,
down the River Nile,
his canoe gently rocking.

IV.
From time to time,
my granddaddy tells me,
the bulb flickered off,
the warmth leaking
from the shack,
his story in tributaries and rivulets
of fractal light.

Flowers in April

ANNA SUDDERTH, Grade 11, Age 17. Trinity Valley School, Fort Worth, TX, Lucas Jacob, *Educator*

Purple giraffes,
as my mother called the stacked
blossoms of henbit, had a tendency
to appear suddenly,
overnight. I would go to sleep
on a dry evening and

the next day, there would be rain
that made the newly sprouted henbit smell
sharp, green, and I would run
in my navy-blue third-grade uniform
from mound to mound with no jacket because
it wasn't cold, just wet,

and I would lie in the henbit,
and I would let their sage-like
blossoms, laced with water, touch
my skin, and in my head
I would write poems, long and full
of adjectives, describing so
many things:

the echoing sound of April rain
after my grandfather's death,

the heartiness
of inky irises in the flower-bed,

the lick of the grass,
the coolness of my own lips,
the soft surprise of how warm
the rain was, how gentle on my dry feet, my hair.

The Two O's of Eyes

WARREN KENNEDY-NOLLE, Grade 7, Age 13. Rye Country Day
School, Rye, NY, Anne Alexander, *Educator*

At the testing hour,
across sunset rocks, skimming gypsum dunes,

still the missile screams

The geckos gawk, all tongue and blink
A fox fritters across fronds of ocotillo . . .

Are they ever used to this?

But under Alamogordo rocks, creatures once crawled
Overlooked by Fat Man

Indifferent to all eyes.
What was it to O'Keefe?
Where the calla lily stands, a pigmented pallet
Its quirky colors squiggled from dried tubes,
dusted undaunted
by the dune's blessing.
Georgia is finding water
amid prickly pears, yucca stalks
Missile base; The White Place?

Oppenheimer strikes that Plaza Blanca spirit
In porkpie hat, scouting for the best site.
Remembering his horses, he returns
to the brick-like Alamos canyons.

Soon just a P.O. Box, crammed
with censored letters to the New Look ladies,

wives fawning over Oppie at the cocktail parties . . .
Uranium dust under his nails,
Maybe he'll glow in the dark,

Nothing else to do,
After the day's calculations mount,
making it all add up in math and morals.

How would she paint that mushroom?
She has no Little Boy
Her canvas stays blank,
Late Abiquiu afternoons
with a chosen few
To talk to on the patio,
over her nicely landscaped
bomb shelter.

Her brush; his switch
In death and loss,
where is Trinity the cross
Is it nothing?

After the grass grows gray
And Japan bakes black,
It's all Ghost Ranch.

Ever the missile,
the last to see
When the dunes don white,
The temperate snowflakes
fallout
Scouring the winter wind
The endless embers
melting all touch.

New Year, After You Go

EMELINE ATWOOD, Grade 12, Age 17. Milton Academy, Milton, MA,
James Connolly, *Educator*

The Maasai give mothers one day
to grieve, death then left unassisted. No
funerals, no ceremonies, just Ngai,
their god who takes evil out past
bomas to the reddest parts of Tarangire
and brings back goodness,
black and blessed, to the people.

When sadness comes home to sit like tea,
the shofar blows, hot and breath-heavy,
so we reflect. Autumn drums down its leaves, and one death
recalls the next. Our house hangs,
suspended. We fold sandwich bags
back in the box, leave tomatoes
rotting in the fridge. No longer
do we throw things out—we won't risk missing them.
At night, our father fumbles with the
answering machine, trying to erase your voice
yet hold it in his palm. Sun dials spin
out rainbows on our bedroom wall. In the mornings,
our mother's rowing machine creaks us awake. Sun checkers
my covers with light, the sounds of a soundless house
massaging the wooden floor
back and forth.

Our mother says even young people die. She says grief halts
only those who let it.

In the kitchen, I tie my hair
to chop the carrots, feel some faith that isn't mine.
I am Apache with blue eyes, my mother's
Moses and father's Christ tangled
within me. I grew up Hebrew,
then Jesus, then nothing.

No tribe, no tradition, no God.
No Laiboni to absolve me
of grunge. So, like moonlight, sadness slides in
through the staircase railings
when I'm the last up. It doesn't drop
away to desert, but leaves me
wandering.

I wish I grew up with church,
even synagogue. My mother hands me apples with honey
and tells me to eat. I try to find the faith she forgot
to give. The matzo balls are brewing,
and Tishri comes slow as warriors. They hike
along the desert edge through lion grass,
their backs to sun. Light,
hot and humming, falls through the ceiling fixtures.
I look up until it spots my eyes,
look up until little angels
dance in them.

Saba, Grandfather

ELIZABETH HEYM, Grade 12, Age 17. Bexley High School, Bexley, OH,
Chad Hemmelgarn, *Educator*

Take me back to the Negev,
where you once told me that the desert blooms,
that the weathered fingertips of our heritage reached
across years in which we wandered on pavement that was not
ours,
reached to touch the sandy supine palm of our land.

We knelt on the simmering earth, warm as hands
clasped for hours on the crowded streets of Beersheba.
We opened up the land with trowels.
In the shine of the sand-swarmed surface I could see your face,
downturned eyes, eyebrows like the slope of
meandering sand meeting the Mediterranean,
as your body reverently bent over the land.

You told me that we must dig a hole to plant a tree,
that a land must fall before it may rise,
must be carved and empty before finding roots.

As I fly away, the warm surface of Israel panning, swelling
over the airplane's wing, you watch the sky,
hoping I realize
you were speaking about more than the land.

The Heliades Search for Phaethon

MADELEINE LECESNE, Grade 11, Age 17. Lusher Charter School, New Orleans, LA, Brad Richard, *Educator*

We wept until the ground grew supple
and slipped beneath the earth,
searching for our brother in the dark tunnels,
surrounded by broken bones.
We found his right hand and took turns
holding it against our cheeks. It was warm
with callouses. Pieces of Phaethon, disbanded,
scattered inside the ground.
We had to find every one.
I wept as I crawled.

We were only with our brother in darkness.
Aboveground the sky was darker
than these tunnels. Helios couldn't
let any light beat through from heaven.
Earth was meant to live as Phaethon lives now. We had already
   forgotten
about the light, and our bones weakened
from being in the black too long.
As we collected the last pieces
of our brother,
our grief fossilized,
and our tears turned golden.
We took his parts, skin
just barely holding on

to the bones, and pushed
ourselves upward, germinating
and flourishing into Poplars
as we broke Earth, alive
and reaching toward Helios.
Our amber tears kept slipping.

Will

SARAH GAMARD, Grade 12, Age 18. New Orleans Center for Creative Arts, New Orleans, LA, Lara Naughton, *Educator*

Your name tastes like bread,
like water on the roof of my mouth, like July rain
making sewing thread on robin egg houses.
~~ouch: stiff and familiar,
scarred by fingernails and ballpoint pens.
Your arms are bread, ropes and fishnets, worn and
constricting.
Your hair is an Indian river, your stubble the krill of the ocean.
Your name is bread. Your body is bread.
Your shirts smell like cheap vanilla candles, like blankets for a
crying child, like aerosol.
Your toes are sugar cubes, cavaliers on my legs.
Your nose is a mouse, soft and burrowing into the corners of
my neck, a boat. You are bread, anger sculpted by an artist.
You are salt. Nostalgia.
The dry shore of Alabama, the white sand
that pales my feet and squeaks underneath me,
the rainbow umbrella, coarse towel and plastic chair.
Will, you are cucumbers in June.
Your voice is a barn in the afternoon.
You are hay and snakes in stables, shoes kicking up sawdust,
the water from a hose.
You are bread. White bread. The bread toddlers bring to ponds.
Bread crumbs on the bills of mallards, making ripples on
water.
You are tire grease, cloth car seats, long rides on the interstate
to Texas,

creaking furniture and spongy paint.
You are swallows in the rafters of supermarkets,
squirrels splashing in a bird bath,
springtime puddles in parking lots.
Your eyes are black singers, screamers, stained-glass windows
in the holy morning.
Your back is that of a horse climbing the trails of Appalachia,
carrying the weight of men, shoulders rubbing and rolli
under a leather saddle.
Will, you feel like the earth.
Your ankles are mountains east of the Mississippi River.
The scars on your skin taste like bread.
The stitch marks on your forehead,
just above your eyebrow, the shape of a seagull's wing,
are soil to the tree roots of my fingers.

Zeniths and Nadir

ASHLEY HUANG, Grade 10, Age 15. Klein Oak High School, Spring, TX,
Jo Gauen, *Educator*

I am remembering a grade-school project
involving the raising of birds, fledgling

mourning doves, warm buds of hope
under the fingers, solitary hearts

that clench and sputter and release.
I am remembering

an idle comment once made, yours, when young:
"the sun is the closest star."

I have long since learned
that dreams are the heaviest burdens. Our shoulders

are now cramped from carrying the weight
of that, the strain of another sleepless dawn.

From continuously rubbing contentment out,
breaking the skin on our blisters, going from callow

to callous. I am remembering
Icarus and his father,

a canted smear of rust and cloud,
a skimming of wingtips across an event

horizon, the nodding skid and sink
of the prodigal son. We have traced his arc of stars,

eighteen years and counting, hoping our wings
are less wire, less wax, more blood, marrow, muscle.

This is what they give us to work with.
We must all make do.

I am remembering
the promise you made me, tired

to the bone the night before graduation, that we
are no Icarus, no shudder of heat across

a milk-and-water sky. That we are much more
than our zeniths and nadirs.

I am remembering
those last few months brushing past, bathwater

wicked from the feathers of geese, loose
and lazy. Here is one more fatal summer, air shrill

with the chirrs of sunrise, our palms upturned to cradle the
coming day.

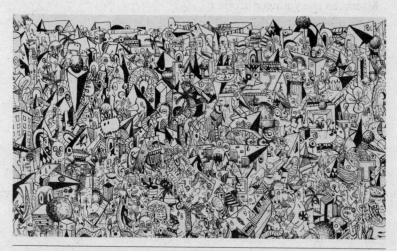

TANNER RHINES, *Black and White Compression, Part 1*, Grade 12, Age 18.
West Valley High School, Fairbanks, AK. Kris Haggland, *Educator.*
2014 American Visions Medal

Miami as a Household

DALIA AHMED, Grade 11, Age 16. Miami Arts Charter School,
Miami, FL, Jen Karetnick, *Educator*

I.
Miami as the younger brother
is dysfunctional in this family of tropical cities.
He is still adolescent and a late bloomer,
loud—his voice cracking with Cuban thunder.
A canopy of dreams hangs from his wingspan,
hands deep in the pockets of a palm frond,
wrenching the life from its seams.

II.
Miami as the Dominican maid
has culture camped in her collarbone
and hides crumbs of Cuban bread
in the pocket of her apron.
She is a dialect of her own: thick like *yuca*.
Her scent carries a bouquet of hibiscus,
breath tinged with the strength of red tea.

III.
Miami as a mother is armed with weeds
and history clogged in the roots of a mangrove.
She is a native tongue thick with soil.
Arms feeding violent currents, she is hurricane
woman: all voice, claps of thunder, a skirt of wind
unfurling seeds.

Picking Favorites

AILEEN MA, Grade 12, Age 17. Providence High School, Charlotte, NC, Marva Hutchinson, *Educator*

You taught me how to love mangoes,
how to peel back the
smooth leathery skin and reveal
the juicy flesh within,
saturated with sugar and
sunshine.
You taught me how to pick
the biggest and ripest fruit,
taught me to eat them quickly
before the flesh rots away.

You taught me to love mangoes,
but you also taught me how to
hate you for feeding me mangoes while
feeding my mother the idea that
she's not good enough,
that single-handedly raising two daughters
is not enough to earn your respect.

I hated you for mocking her religion,
her prayers to a distant god
whose presence is holy and
welcome in our household.

You are not allowed to complain
about me not honoring my father.
You lost the right to complain about my criticism
when you started criticizing my mother

for everything she did,
when you started to dominate over her
actions and chastising her indecisions,
when you forced her to tolerate you
and your crude behavior,
the remnants of your childhood in the
dirt-covered streets of China.

She still loved you
until she found the strength
to see you as spotted and
rotted and
gone.

You taught me to love mangoes,
but my mother taught me to love all fruits
no matter how sweet
or how sour,
no matter how prickly the surface
or how difficult to peel open.
You taught me to pick the ripest fruit,
but my mother taught me
how to see through the perfect exterior
and spot the rotten cores.

You taught me how to form a thick skin,
to cultivate a hard, bitter seed.

But Mother taught me
to keep a soft heart and an open mind,
to have a tough skin for protection
from men like you—
not from knowledge and understanding
and forgiveness.

So when my mother asks me
to prepare a fresh mango
for the two of us,
I think of the sweet sunshine
in my mother's laugh,
the one I have not heard in years.

Journal

HADASSAH AMANI, Grade 8, Age 12. Miami Arts Charter School, Miami, FL, Jen Karetnick, *Educator*

I love to feel the sweet tickle
of her hand gliding across my pages.
She knows what she does to me.

Her words are almost magical.
It's the way she writes to me
that sends a little tingle down my spine.

Aesthetic love letters.
Poetry.
Songs.

But she hasn't written today.
Not yet. I begin to fear
I'm being replaced.

I remain solitary
and await the light rustling
of my leaves. But when she does

write again, her letters seem unfamiliar.
I begin to wonder if she was ever
writing to me or if I was just . . .

eavesdropping.

From Penelope, to Odysseus Lost at Sea

ZOE CHENG, Grade 11, Age 16. Walnut Hills High School, Cincinnati, OH, Francesca Bownas-Rayburn, *Educator*

The olives are ready for harvest.
Hard and salty like little boys' fingers.
Gnarled trees with white arms
standing like sentinels. Night comes and
I dream of citadels and plunder.

Waves stain the windows with
their morning breath. Creep into my bed
like lusting gods;
nothing here is completely dry anymore.

The suitors around the fire eat our lambs and
the fat drips down their cheeks. They
drink our wine and the vomit flows
from their mouths.
Both of these things help the fire burn.

Sometimes, when they catch
me watching, they laugh and
tell me you are dead.

Here is the truth.
I wish you were dead.

Two days ago, I shattered
an amphora. Wine, ruby-red,
licked and buried itself

into the white marble.
It shocked me. I could've
sworn that daggers had
flown through my heart.
The wine looked so like blood.
I pretended I was cleaning
your blood from the floor.

The night is blacker here.
I cannot remember if it has always been so black.
Perhaps your blood has
sunk into the sky like
bones into wet dirt. Or
the waves have dampened the clouds
like a drunkard will spoil his
own chiton.

Either way, the product remains.
Things are blacker where
the soul dips into ink.

A Lesson on Astronomy

KYNA SMITH, Grade 10, Age 15. Cab Calloway School of the Arts,
Wilmington, DE. Jill Protokowicz, *Educator*

The moon is beautiful.
She's been asking about you.

Despite her beauty,
she chooses to hide parts of herself every night.

I am thinking of your body:
The stitching
of your veins
has been pulled apart . . .

Your hands,
stained with constellations.
We are
glazing the sky,
melting into something easy to spill.

Galaxies seep through my bones;
I wish to be fluent in this touch.

I am thinking of your body:
A lover,
saying darling, I don't know how to love you correctly.
Your honey haze,
trembling with absolution.

The moon is beautiful, her craters
remind me
that something full of light
can also be hollow.

Bad Dumpling

JACKIE YANG, Grade 12, Age 17. King High School, Tampa, FL,
Mark Pollard, *Educator*

A-yi is clumsy with her words. Her eager conversations are
filled with malapropisms and glaring mispronunciations that
blindly stumble over each other, her sentences punctuated
with excited inhales that exhaust her listeners more than herself. The rolling rhythm of her speech harmonizes well with
the gurgling pot of boiling water on the stove.

"Make-ah a little wet with the wah-ter. Make sticky."

She draws out the first syllable of water so that the word itself lilts, leaping up and back down like a raindrop in a puddle.
Little Jimmy eagerly finger-paints wet patterns on his circle of
thin, powdered dough.

A-yi lets out a laugh, a shrill, juvenile giggle that trails in the
air for two seconds longer than it should. "No-ah, like this."
She dips her thin finger into the porcelain bowl, wetting it just
enough to trace the edges of the circle of dough. A quarter-
sized dollop of sticky ground meat mixed with spinach and
scallions is spooned into the middle of the circle. A-yi folds the
flour up like a small taco, then slowly pinches and twists the
wet edges with her fingers until the dumpling is fully sealed.

"Why won't it work?" Jimmy's face twists into a familiar expression that is usually a harbinger for tears. His dumpling is limp, and bits of ground meat are spilling out at the seams.

A-yi laughs again. "Too much meat-ah! Here." Jimmy is appeased as she fixes his lopsided dumping; a meltdown has been averted.

A-yi tosses the batch of dumplings into the pot, and the boiling water roars angrily as each infant-like crescent plops in. We resume our work at the dinner table while it cooks.

The wooden surface is covered with flour and rolls of smooth, creamy dough. A-yi slices each roll into elastic discs, which we roll around in our small palms and flatten against the tabletop until they become perfectly thin, round circles. As we slap them onto the table, the unsettled flour kisses our tan arms and our dark hair and A-yi's secondhand copy of *The Official Guide to the TOEFL Test* on the corner of the table. Whether she is cooking or sleeping, that ratty blue book never seems to be far from her reach.

I never asked her why. I did ask my mother once, while I was begrudgingly clearing my old study of its heavy science textbooks and political autobiographies so it could be fashioned into a new guest bedroom, why her sister, at age thirty-five, had suddenly decided to abandon a doctorate at the University of Hong Kong in order to move halfway across the world to study at a Floridian community college.

My mother vaguely told me that her sister was experiencing marital problems and wanted a new beginning. I turned back to my books to see Hillary Clinton looking up at me with a wry smile, chin on fist, as if curious as to why anyone in her right mind would make such a myopic decision.

I wipe my brow carefully with the edge of my hand. "Is that test hard?" I jerk my chin to the direction of her book. When I get up to use the restroom at night, I often find her still awake studying. Through the crack of her doorway, I can see her hunched over her dog-eared book, determinedly memorizing verbs and gerunds and prepositional phrases by the dim light of her desk lamp.

A-yi shrugs. "It okay." Another embarrassed laugh. "Sometimes it confusing-ah, a little." Her hands shift nimbly across the surface of the dumpling, a seamstress stitching rows of neat pleats in an ivory skirt of dough.

"Why do we have to use meat in dumplings? I want to put cheese in mine!" Jimmy shrieks.

"Ah, you cannot mix Western food with Chinese dumpling, that is yucky dumpling!" My aunt's dramatically disgusted face evokes a jovial giggle from Jimmy. "No one want to eat your bad dumpling-ah."

My dumplings are misshapen; some are too obese, others are too meager. My edges look more like clumsy dimples than skirt pleats. I smack a spoonful of pink meat into the center and blurt out, "Why did you move here, anyways?"

A-yi lowers her eyes and doesn't answer immediately. The pot on the stove boils over, demanding her immediate attention. She turns down the heat and fishes out the dumplings from the steaming water with a mesh skimmer. They are tan and tender, glistening with moisture. After they dry out, the skins will look semi-translucent. My mouth waters at the sight of them.

"I just meant to say—it seems like it would be a lot easier to just stay in China to study." My fingers clumsily knock over the rolling pin. It clatters to the floor.

A-yi picks it up and moves to wash it in the sink. "You remember my husband?" She's talking in Cantonese now. Her voice is leveler, her rhythm fluid. Her syllables have stopped stumbling, now politely toe-heeling in an orderly line. Jimmy can't understand a word, but he's too occupied with crafting mutant dumplings to be curious.

I think about the few times I've seen my uncle during family visits. He is a small man with a receding hairline, as pale and as dimpled as the dumpling cupped in my palm. In pictures, he often wears white short-sleeved button-downs, tucked into a pair of belted slacks, his small black eyes guarded by the white glare of his rectangular wire-frame glasses. "I remember."

"He is a very smart man. He graduated at the top of his class from Peking University." A-yi rinses the rolling pin under the faucet, the water carving rivulets into its floury patina. "Peking University is the top school in China, kind of like the Harvard of China."

"Wah, I didn't know that."

"He was always very smart, very intelligent. Every time he spoke, he spoke as if he knew exactly what he was talking about." She laughs, but it's much softer than her usual theatrical caw. "His confidence was what drew my attention to him in the first place."

I move my hands back and forth, stretching and folding the edge of my dumpling in the closest imitation of A-yi's movements. I remember how my uncle's clear voice would quiet all other conversation at our family dinner table, its low register and sporadic rhythm announcing its own expertise. I was only a toddler and couldn't understand a word of what he was saying, but there was an insistency in his tone that carried me with its current.

The rows of dumplings on our tray are slowly growing, lined up against each other like virgin-skinned newborns in a nursery. I am gleeful to see that the distinction between my dumplings and A-yi's is lessening.

"I thought that I really had the luck, getting to marry a smart graduate from Peking University. I married young, right out of college. We were in love."

I can't help but smile. It seems surreal to hear this small woman, whose twiggy, angular limbs still possess the adolescent awkwardness of someone still learning to embrace her skin, speak of being in love.

"I learned so many things from him. He was very attentive to me and liked to teach me new things in his free time, and I discovered that he really was brilliant." A-yi sighs, slapping a dumpling skin a couple of times in the flour. "Because he was so intelligent and had great credentials, he had an authority that commanded respect and obedience from everybody. If he took one step, he expected the ground around him to shift for miles. Like a giant."

A-yi's voice sounds tired. Our tray has filled again, and she dumps this batch into the pot. Jimmy yelps at the loud gush of water that greets the dumplings. "He said he would be a very busy man with his new government post, so I quit my part-time job at a pharmaceutical company for a while. I just stayed at home to take care of him, but I was new at being a wife and did not seem to do anything right, no matter how hard I tried. One time I saved some of my best char siu pork on the table for his dinner, since he was working very late, and I came back into the kitchen that night to see him scraping everything off his plate into the trash. He told me that he simply did not care for char siu pork." A-yi clucks her tongue. "Can you believe it? He just expected the world to shift around to meet his needs, because he did not think he could ever be wrong."

The rubbery ball of dough sandwiched between my palms rolls between my fingers, and I think of Mr. Hawthorne, my wizened first-period English teacher who makes a sadistic show of tearing apart papers handed in without his correct NAME-DATE-SUBJECT-PERIOD heading on the upper-right-hand corner. "My way or the highway!" he'll bark. "My way or the highway!"

A-yi laughs again when I tell her the phrase in English. "My way or the highway-ah?" She tests the syllables, rolling them around her tongue as if tasting a foreign dish. "Why that mean something?"

I explain it to her in Cantonese, and she nods knowingly. "Yes, exactly. That is the kind of person he was. He expects you to get out of his way if you are not going to play by his rules. At first, he was very supportive of me going back to school. But then he was always calling me during class because he needed me to do something for him while he was busy with his job, and I would always have to leave early or be tardy to complete his emergency errands. Whenever I told him I absolutely could not help, he got very irritated."

"That's very—egocentric." I can't remember the Cantonese term.

"Egocentric?"

I nod. "Ego is a Latin root, it means yourself. Centric means centered around, revolving around. It's important to learn roots like that for your TOEFL. It makes remembering words easier."

"Roots?" A-yi nods slowly as she flattens out her circle of dough.

"Yes. I can help you if you'd like. Study for the test." I steal a cooked dumpling from the platter on the counter. The first bite through the elastic skin is steaming and juicy. I gulp down the remainder, ignoring my scalding tongue.

"Thank you, you're such a kind child," A-yi says with a shy smile as her hands continue to pleat a dumpling skin in a continuous pattern of folding and pressing, folding, pressing. "I never thought it would be so difficult to start over in a new place. There's so many things to learn; I am so behind. It is very embarrassing when my English professors are younger than me! And people keep using expressions that I do not understand, like well that's a wrap." A-yi enunciates the words with an over-affectation. "The other day, the leader of our study group said it, and I had no idea what he meant until the others began to leave."

She finishes sealing her dumpling and reaches over to help Jimmy with one of his. "But it is going to be good for me now. There is so much room here in America, room for your single-family homes and your wide blue horizons. I have room for my own priorities here. With my husband in China, everything was about him. I had to keep on shifting my life and my interests around because he was always more important. Eventually, I realized that I couldn't shift myself around like this anymore. My husband was too gigantic, and that left no room for me." A-yi shrugs. "So I moved here."

"I see," I murmur. I think of Audrey, my best friend since third grade, who has gotten into a habit of appeasing and apologizing around her stormy-faced boyfriend, whom she claims is "sensitive and misunderstood." Last week, she broke down in the girl's bathroom and sobbed into a wad of bargain tissue paper after he gave her the cold shoulder for who-knows-what. My loud, brazen friend full of laughter had been reduced to a sniffly, docile, plain-vanilla shell of herself—a meatless dumpling.

Jimmy adds the last dumpling to the batch, and I take them to cook. They bob up and down in the bubbling water like carefree babies in a hot tub, completely relieved of the knowledge that they'll soon perish in the acidic depths of our stomachs. Jimmy wears a funny face as he watches me sift out the dumplings, like he's trying to hold in one of his number twos. He eventually can't contain himself and bursts out in a mischievous giggle.

"What you laughing at-ah, Jee-my?" A-yi turns around in her chair.

Jimmy points to the packet of Kraft shredded cheese on the counter. "I added cheese to my dumplings! Cheese dumplings!" He lets out a full belly laugh, congratulating himself for outsmarting us.

"Yucky!" A-yi shakes her head.

Nevertheless, we take a seat and prepare to feast. I take my pick of the platter carefully, examining each dumpling for unnatural tints of orange.

"Do you miss your husband?" I ask A-yi in English as I sink my teeth into a perfectly average dumpling.

A-yi nods. "A little-ah. He can be very sweet and-ah caring, sometime. That's why I love him, first. But I then discover that—that though he be nice on the surface, there is something under that, in his spirit, you know, that was not so good-uh. Something that I could not see. Something—ah!" She spits out a mouthful of mush and melted cheese. "Bad dumpling."

The Survivor

AUSTIN WEI, Grade 8, Age 13. Lakeside Middle School, Seattle, WA, Susie Mortensen, *Educator*

Prologue: Central Kalimantan, Borneo

A thin yet seizing Equatorial mist grasps hold of the emerald mass: the Borneo rainforest, a giant tucked between swirling seas. Through minute gaps in the canopy, pockets of radiance slip through, torches flickering in a lively dungeon. Amidst the howls, squeaks, and rustles of the forest, vibrant with life, a village shaman treads through the moist brush foraging for herbs, a weary but keen stare spread narrowly across his eyes. Lost on an unfamiliar route, he lets out a hoarse grunt of annoyance, as he struggles to gauge the direction. One misstep leads his balance to falter, and he stumbles over a protruding root, torso smacking the damp earth. Struggling to get back up, he raises his head and suddenly—dwindling vision, sunset sky, leech-infested marsh seem to disappear as he visualizes a bizarre sight, looming like a phantom before him.

The distinctive hull of a riverboat comes into view, with fading paint ghostly white, immobilized in the sluggish marsh. Why does it linger here, miles away from any river route? A deluge of overwhelming curiosity suppresses the shaman's anxiety as he trots forth to get a better view. But what he witnesses next plunges his mind into insanity: a body brimming with the venom of sickness and infested with blood-filled blisters, a ravaged human being bordering death, lying conspicuously on the deck. The horror smashes the shaman, like a stake drilled into his core, and the most primeval of instincts sends him bursting through the jungle.

* * *

The whir of a helicopter wing disturbs the evening breeze, as the aircraft descends cautiously upon the uneven clearing. The tall grass squeaks underneath as the men file out silently, clad in gear fit for outer space: thick white suits complete with bulky masks, eliminating all contact with the outside. The peculiar expedition marches through the unwelcome branches, buzzing with the sounds of insects chirping to the moon, the birds fleeing by shrieking as if in annoyance. "There," whispers the leader, pointing to the bog in front of the cohort, the beams from his flashlight pointing out a rickety boat. As the group trudges into the shallow river under the starry sky, one can easily notice their grave expressions even through tinted glass visors.

* * *

Hospital in Samarinda City Emergency Ward #26
His eyes twitch back and forth beneath their lids, nightmares swirling into the dizzying vortex of black and white. The bustle of frantic doctors is close by, but seems far off—sounds from an outlandish world whizzing into his eardrums. Stripped of reality, his senses are merged into one: hearing, smell, touch, even the taste in the sour cavity of his mouth, tangle into a ramshackle heap laid before his mind. In fits of hallucination, a cloud materializes in dense lumps hovering around the sole survivor, like a soggy veil of fog in the familiar rainforest. But surprisingly, it is not composed of vapor, but by the very build-

ing blocks of himself. The mist swirls, circling, reverberating with his most cherished possessions, thoughts, memories, emotions . . . all piled together, sucked into an overwhelming whirlpool, deeper, deeper . . . unreachable and drowned in the vacuum of the man's mind.

With a heaving impulse, the sickly man's subconscious forces him to lunge forward. The next moment, his chest is lifted inches from the bed's bondage and the frightened doctors backpedal for a few steps, sirens buzzing, secretions exuding from the patient's frail body. Shuffling of feet, and a panicked struggle to regain control arises like a tempest, while numbness plummets onto his mind again. Without word or reason, the paralyzing darkness descends, and the survivor's weak conscience is switched off like a lamp, a trance that suffocates his soul.

* * *

Empty Room: Reality or Hallucination?

A wooden stool casts an elongated shadow, splayed across the barren concrete. The squeak of the stool's failing leg resonates across the space, a nasty cackle that seems to broil the man's heart as he sits upon it, setting the ambience of an unfamiliar realm. A stooped figure is silhouetted against the dim-lit wall, arms crossed before his chest, a hazy shadow across the bare room. The survivor is buried in the fearful atmosphere, entrenched in an icy blanket of terror. The unbearable impulsion emerges from his quivering lips, words stumbling out of his mouth, "Who . . . are . . . you?"

In a voice darker than the underworld, deeper than the ocean trenches, the shadow replies in what could only be described as woefulness laced with rage, "You know me." And as if to punctuate his presence, repeats the dreaded words, "You know me."

* * *

"With that catch we got yesterday, we're sure to make a fortune. Those wealthy folk will definitely be glad to have their new pets. Only one more 'baby' left to fill our order." Agung was always jovial, the most flamboyant speaker of our group by any measure. He was our leader who never failed, managing catch after catch successfully. Guntur enthusiastically expressed his agreement while I looked on wordlessly, mumbling half-hearted approval. Holding the helm, the river was my only focus . . .

* * *

The silhouette is deathly silent, waiting for the man's response. The words had launched forth into the air like a dust storm whisking past a sand dune. Indignant, the man's deep fear forces his mouth to sputter, "I don't know you . . . you've got the wrong man. I don't know you, I don't recognize you and . . . and . . . just go away." The last words emerge out of a rising panic through his shrieking voice.

* * *

It was deep into the afternoon, and the sun was fast approaching the western hills as we trudged through the undergrowth. The humid breeze and the incessant rattling of the rainforest were behind us. Armed with weapons and traps, we charged toward the treetop, legs bursting from the thicket, after the furry prize . . .

* * *

In reply, the figure raises his deep voice, ranting in bitter words, "How do you not know me? You invaded our home, massacred our clan, enslaved our young, and feasted on our demise. That is who you are, a murderous poacher. I know you, I understand you to the heart of your evil mind. I know you . . . how dare you not know me?"

* * *

The nurse peeks into the horrific room through the opening of the door, a thin crevasse barely an inch wide. There lies the dreadful man, fingers occasionally fidgeting, but otherwise quiet and immobile. His body is laid out awkwardly on the chalk-white bed, guarded within a quarantine cell, like a grotesque corpse, horrific to any eye. Glancing at the machines to at least fulfill her errand, the nurse leaps out immediately, as if the sheer presence of the room is contagious.

* * *

The rest of the clan had retreated, and their frightful faces gazed back from the vibrating grove, weeping distantly over the carnage. The mother was lying sideways, fur moistened by the bloody puddle, barely breathing through damaged lungs, wounded beyond repair. Yet still, the orangutan clutched her child with one uninjured arm. Agung gave a chuckle, "I guess we've filled our order." He bent down with two hands to pry open the grasp, eyes fixated on the treasure . . . The event occurred suddenly, an impossibly rapid motion—the mother lurched up with the final sap of her strength, opened her jaws wide, snapping down blade-sharp teeth, blood swelling instantly out of Agung's wrist. Unsure of what to do, Guntur rushed in blindly to help. Met by the same menacing canines, he jerked back with a yelp, a fine cut oozing crimson across his outstretched arm. Yelling for my partners to back off, I fired a bullet from my rifle . . . and at last, the beast had met its end.

* * *

The head doctor looks up from his cluttered desk, meeting the eyes of a well-dressed man who had just entered his office. In a youthful but experienced voice, he introduces himself briskly as an investigator of the Health Department, sent down from Jakarta. Dr. Sanjaya, as is shown on the plaque of his office door, knows instantly what the man is here for. He comments, "You want to speak with the patient in Ward 26, I presume."

The agent replies, "Ah, yes. I was told he was diagnosed with Makassarese fever. The department is gravely concerned and we want to find out what happened immediately. We're quite puzzled about this plague. There hasn't been an outbreak for the last 50 years, I believe. Is he available right now?"

Dr. Sanjaya replies grimly, "He has not regained consciousness, and I don't believe he will for at least a week. You should plan for a long stay."

The agent grimaces, "I see. Are there any reports of who this person is?"

The doctor, apologetically continues, "Sorry . . . we don't know anything about him."

* * *

I had barely the strength to bury them after their terrible suffering. I felt horrified, watching their once energetic faces deprived of life. They were the faces that I had known for so long, that I have even forgotten when we first met. Piling pebbles in a pattern that spelled out their names on top of two mounds of dirt, rocks trembling in my frail palm, Agung and Guntur were laid to rest, at peace in the autumn mist. With what energy I could summon, I climbed, or more like clambered, aching and starved, into the damp riverboat. Dizzy and choking, I felt the fever that I had tried so hard to avoid sweep over me like a filthy mop. I started the engine strenuously, my strength flooding out, and I tumbled hazily into a daydream, the dreadful image of the beast's ferocious mouth pegged in time. That was when I sobbed, when I tried to make sense of it all, the heinousness of the orangutan, and the poison of its mouth. That was when I witnessed its savagery, when I tried to expel it with my weakened mind, but couldn't.

* * *

Irate and insulted, the poacher leaps forward from the chair in anger. The splintered wood scratches the cement, a sound more ear-splitting than a bat's shriek. He shouts in reply, with as much rage as he can harness, "I am a poor man desperately trying to make ends meet. I have not committed a single crime against a fellow human being, and I value their life the same as I value my own. I have watched two friends perish beside me, killed by the filthy jaws of an orangutan, and I am suffering, almost ready to join them in another world. That is who I am, how dare you accuse me of murder!"

The ensuing silence is peculiar, and for the first time the shadow starts to move. Before the poacher's eyes, it turns sluggishly, as if weary, facing the man and straightening up its stature, with a hood obscuring its head, cranking upwards. In words rising in a tremolo of dread, ringing like a migraine across the poacher's brain, the shadow's speech is the impersonation of darkness, a peril that could consume any light, extinguish any hope, "I have all the right to accuse you!" And swiftly, the hood sweeps back, unveiling the figure's giant head, expanding until it comprises all of the poacher's conscience. Orange fur, bared jaws. An orangutan, lunging forth toward him. The sound comes so violently as to defy reality: the orangutan roars not like the picturesque display of a lion, unbridled and pompous, but something choked, a cry through bloodshot eyes and mournful teardrops, "You will pay for our loss . . . you will pay . . . with your life!"

* * *

The ward is utterly muted, save for the whirring of life support machines. It would make anyone wonder if life could possibly exist in its grip . . . until the spasms emerge. They erupt suddenly and without warning, hurtling the man's limbs about. The patient's body resembles smoldering ashes, transforming into a conflagration. That dreadful movement, like the bothersome nagging of an alarm clock—leads it all to happen. Cacophony erupts, sirens buzz, doctors dash, scramble, shout, panic . . .

* * *

The commotion settles, as doctors continue to work over the man in the adjacent room, the sudden panic alleviated as the patient lives on but in deeply worsened condition. The investigator returns to the office, pushing the door ajar, and inquiring urgently, "Will you be able to save him?"

Dr. Sanjaya casts a grim look toward the floor of polished tile. Somberly, he begins, "He's still alive but under weakened condition. The chances are too slim to estimate and his heart might stop at any moment. Sorry, but that's the only information I can offer you."

The agent sinks his head as he replies with a sigh, "I guess if he doesn't live, we won't know if the plague is going to be with us. We'll never know what happened."

The doctor agrees with a slight nod, a grieving voice tapering off, "Yeah, I guess we'll never know . . ."

* * *

Epilogue

The storm burgeons suddenly. Ebony clouds blacken the sunlight, shrouding the rainforest in a torrential downpour. The putrid corpses tumble out of their ruined graves. Agung and Guntur, still cringing in their sickness, which had ridden them of life, are washed pale on the riverbank, a mass of rotten flesh floating like weathered logs into the raging floods.

Sunrise slices through the clouds and the forest is the same as it has been all along, tall and daunting with mighty trees alongside rich soil. A riverboat, engine crooning in the haze, whisks into the deep jungle. A deckhand shouts out, "I think I spotted a corpse back there." A chuckling reply behind him, "Don't worry about it, must be some dead animal." Up the stream they venture, into the territory of the orangutan, the elusive treasure that they seek . . .

* * *

Finally Getting It

RONA WANG, Grade 10, Age 15. Lincoln High School, Portland, OR, Emily Hensley, *Educator*

My brother wouldn't let me into his treehouse, 'cause it was no-girls-allowed. Him and Jimmy and Cheeser and Suzon-not-Susan were all afraid that I'd be better at doing boy things than they are, I bet.

Girls don't do boy things not because we can't, but because we aren't stupid enough to, and that's a pretty important distinction, but the Super-Secret-Special-Spies, or whatever they were calling themselves that day, didn't get it.

And all that was, well, I wouldn't say fine, but it was in the grayish muck between okay and lame, and that was good enough to live with.

Until a couple days later, when I saw them unrolling the rope ladder down to let Rosie Anderson in. The girl across the street who was obsessed with horses and even had a pony of her own called Ladybug, even though it sure wasn't anywhere near red-with-black-polka-dots, but Rosie was dumb like that.

She was the kind of girl who wore princess dresses to school, the fancy kind with netting and fur trimming and sparkly shoes to match, even when it wasn't Halloween. And if I tried to pull that kind of thing, I'd get laughed outta second grade, but girls like Rosie got away with a lot more than girls like me.

I stood under the tree even though I didn't care, course not, I was just curious. I heard them initiating her into the Super-Stupid-Sorry-Excuse-of-a-Club circle, with the handshake they got from that ancient movie and the chant that made no sense, 'cause they had their own made-up language that sounded a whole lot like Pig Latin.

Then I left, not mad at all about how they let another girl into the boys-only club but not me. I was totally cool with how Rosie had been kinda my friend since we lived close and now she wasn't, the guys had stolen her. Whatever.

I tried to stomp away, but my shoes made a muffled groaning sound in the grass, and it wasn't loud enough so it just looked like I was squashing beetles.

Later, I asked my brother about why he let Rosie in but not me, but I made sure he knew I didn't actually care, I was just asking to make conversation, and he shrugged. "She's cool. You're not."

And that was that, and a few days later I heard that Rosie and Cheeser were getting married, and he even gave her his best Pokemon card, which meant it was getting really serious, and then another week later they had a big blowout fight over ice cream flavors or something and they were over and Rosie was outta there.

She invited me over to her house the day after, and she told me about the club and how she and them went on secret missions that she had pinky-sworn not to speak 'bout and if she did her parents and her Yorkie and her horsie with the bad name would all die. She told me about how the boys had all run after her during recess like this was some fun thing.

Also, they did her homework for her, she said. And that was pretty annoying, how come my brother couldn't even do the reading packet himself but he gave Rosie a play-by-play of each chapter?

I went home and figured out what was so different between me and Rosie. She had long golden hair that flowed like in the Disney princess movies and mine was short and the color of a mud pie. And she had a horse and I didn't.

The wig was easy enough to find, in Mama's closet where she kept all her old costume stuff back when she was an actress. She was pretty good too, but then she quit.

I scooped up as much of my hair as I could, like the goddesses doing the Oscar-acceptance speeches, and stuck the wig on top. It was more Ariel than Aurora, but it was the best I could do.

The horse was harder, but my brother had this donkey mask that he liked to wear when he was tryin' to impress girls like Rosie. It made him look better, so I could see the logic behind that.

When I came out into the living room, more decked out than a Christmas tree, my brother and Jimmy and Cheeser and Suzon-not-Susan all burst out laughing.

My cheeks felt warm, which was stupid and probably due to the hot fifty-degree-weather. "What?" I demanded. "Haven't you ever seen a girl before?"

"Why're you wearin' a dress?" Suzon-not-Susan demanded in a deep voice that he kept using to be more like a total guy. He was pretty sensitive about that being-a-man stuff, probably since his parents named him something even worse-sounding than Ladybug.

"Rosie wears a dress, and I don't see you playing bad cop with her," I shot back.

"Yeah, maybe, but she's a girl," he said, licking Ritz cracker crumbs off his thumb. "And you're, you know. Not a girl."

"What am I then, a talking houseplant?"

"I think I saw that in some Nickelodeon show," Jimmy piped up helpfully.

"You're like, a guy-girl," Suzon-not-Susan said, as if that made any sense. "Only girls wear dresses."

It was dumb to argue about whether or not I was a girl with a kid who still believed in Santa Claus, so I stomped away, only I was barefoot and our carpet was kitten-fluffy, so it just looked like I cared more about what my brother and his stupid friends had to say than I really did.

A week later Rosie came knocking, because our doorbell was broken again. She was wearing overalls and a baseball cap, and her hair was up in a messy ponytail.

Wait, I had to think. I saw part of a movie like this once, until Mama caught me and never let me go to the video rental store by myself again.

These two kids switched personalities, so the girl started wearing sporty clothes and acting all guy and stuff, which wasn't so bad for her since she was already on the basketball team anyways. But the boy kept acting all prissy since it was the girl's mind inside of his body, so he'd say things like "Oh my goodness" and "I'm loving the Backstreet Boys" and he got teased lots for it.

Was that what had happened to Rosie?

One way to find out. I punched her straight in the nose.

"Ow, ow, ow!" She wheeled around and clutched her face. "What was that for?"

So there wasn't a boy inside her, since a guy would've acted all manly like it didn't hurt at all. Which was good, because I didn't wanna mix our blood together like in the movie. So I asked, "Why are you dressed like that?"

"I was helping Daddy rake leaves," she said proudly, as if this were some super-fun thing. "Anyway, I want you to help me."

I didn't see how I could help her do much. "I dunno the answers to Monday's quiz."

"I wouldn't trust you even if you did." She rolled her eyes, which I'd always wanted to do but wasn't sure how to. I craned my neck back and tried to let my eyeballs bounce around in my head, but I guess my brain was too dense or something, 'cause it didn't work.

"I want you to teach me how to be like you," she said, and then added, "Please. With a cherry on top."

"Why would you want that?" My neck cracked as I rolled my head forward.

She scowled. "I want to do what you do. I want to play soccer at recess time, too. I like running. But for me, I can only run when boys are chasing me. You know?"

I didn't know. "Why don't you just join me and the others on the field next time?"

She shook her head. "It's not that easy."

Now that was new. For girls like her, wasn't everything easy? She could even get my lazy brother to do her homework.

"It's like . . ." She flapped her hands in the air. I'd tried that move before a couple times, but still couldn't fly like Dumbo. "You know why they asked me to join their club?"

"Because you're cool and I'm not?" I guessed.

She glared at me. "What? No! It's because they all wanted to play prince to the damsel in distress. When they went into your room to steal your Halloween candy—"

"What!"

"—they wouldn't even let me join in, because I was too girly and I wasn't supposed to do dangerous things. And they made me marry Cheeser, too, even though his breath always smells like nachos. Because that's what girls like me are supposed to do, they said."

What was I supposed to say to that? I finally settled on, "Huh. Weird. What candy did they take from my stash?"

"Butterfingers, Snickers, Reese's," she said absently. "Can you help me?"

I was still thinking about the stolen candy, and how I was going to stuff my brother's sheets with toothpaste, so I wasn't really thinking when I agreed.

"You know I wanted to be a racecar driver first," Rosie told me some days later. "But Daddy said racecars were for boys and wouldn't I want a pony instead? And then I wanted to name my horsie Lightning because that's so fast, but Daddy said Ladybug was a name a princess would use."

"Your dad has pretty bad taste," I said, trying to see how far I could lean over while sitting crisscross applesauce on her bed without falling off. I tilted too far and tumbled onto the floor.

"He says names are pretty important. He's a writer, so he knows these things. He makes up stuff and gets money. Anyone who's smart enough to get people to pay them to do that is like a genius."

I flung myself back onto her bed, and thought about Suzon-not-Susan and how that made him overly guy, and about Cheeser, who was so embarrassed by his weird unpronounceable foreign name that he went by a lame nickname instead. And about the name Rosie, which even sounded like something a fairy or a pretty girl in those shampoo commercials would be called.

"You're lucky your name is so boring," she said, but not in a mean way. "You don't have to be girly if you don't feel like it." I tried to see if I could do a handstand on her bed. I couldn't.

"Maybe," I said after climbing back up, rubbing my throbbing head. But I couldn't be like Rosie, either, if I wanted to.

I was known as the soccer kid, a guy-girl, and if I tried to change, that wouldn't be so good for me. People like my brother and his friends who thought they knew everything would make fun of me, probably, unless I had magic powers to turn people I didn't like into stone, like in that movie.

"Do you eat dirt?" Rosie then asked me very seriously. I fell off the bed again.

"My other friends say you do, so I shouldn't play with you," she explained, sticking her head down to look at me.

"What's wrong with people who eat dirt?" I didn't, but how was that any of her busy-ness?

"Girls shouldn't eat dirt."

I didn't know why this made me so mad, because it was true, dirt's not so good for the stomach, and I got sick after I tried eating a mud pie my brother made in kindergarten. But suddenly I was just annoyed, at the bed that kept pushing me off and Rosie who wanted to be like me but also wanted me to change even though I didn't eat dirt and Rosie's dumb friends who talked about me when they didn't even know me.

So I left, and made sure to slam the door while I was at it.

That day, I gave Mama back the Ariel wig that had been playing hide-and-seek under my bed with the dust bunnies and a moldy sandwich. Who wanted to be like dumb Rosie Anderson, anyways?

She didn't ask me questions, just jammed it onto her head and spun around the living room. "This was from my first professional play," she said, smiling like there was light inside of her that someone had just switched on. "I was the evil queen."

I always assumed the wig was for a character beautiful and good, like Cinderella maybe. But I guessed it was silly to try to figure out who someone was from just hair.

"Her name was Regina," she continued, which was even weirder since that was a pretty, shampoo-girl type name. "Opening night, I got a standing ovation."

I had to ask, "If you were so good at actress-ing, why'd you quit?"

She slipped the wig off. I squinted at it. It didn't look evil. "I was really good at playing the bad guys."

I frowned, trying to get that sentence. It made less sense than my brother's made-up language.

She saw my face and thought I was being confused not about the meaning of what she said but about why she'd quit. "So that's the only kind of character I got cast as," she explained. "Directors wouldn't let me be anyone else."

I figured acting was a lot like real life.

"Why do you care so much if someone calls you Susan?" I asked Suzon-not-Susan a couple of days later, when he was digging through our fridge to look for popsicles. I didn't bother telling him the Otter Pops would be in the freezer.

Without looking up, he said, "That's not my name. That's a girl name."

"You're no different if you're Suzon or Susan. Or Suzon-not-Susan." I paused. That wasn't totally true. If he'd been named Susan instead when he was born he'd probably get teased lots and that would probably mess him up bad. Susan was a stuffy, oldish name for girls but only because people made it so.

"No, 'cause if I'm Susan then I'm a girl, not a guy-girl like you but a girl. And if I'm a girl then I gotta have long hair and run away from boys."

And because I felt bad for him, I told him, "The Otter Pops are in the freezer, stupid, you're looking in the wrong section."

City Man

CLAY SPACE, Grade 12, Age 17. Eldorado High School,
Albuquerque, NM, Cole Raison, *Educator*

When you get off the plane in Denver, you are no longer Ji-carilla Apache. You are Native American. The first thing you should do is buy a cell phone. Not one of those touch-screen brain-drain devices that can do everything including clip your nails, but one of those cheap flip phones that do what phones are designed to do: call family. Don't get haggled into some expensive monthly plan either, just pay for the minutes. And no, you don't need texting.

Before you call home though, get an apartment. Remember the research you did. Remember that one apartment on Col-fax with the cheap rent, and tell your taxi driver to take you straight there. Don't be tempted to spend money on the way. Don't stop for food at a restaurant, even if you want to. There's plenty of food at the nearby grocery store, just don't expect to find fry bread.

Once you get your apartment, call home. Tell your wife your apartment number so she can mail you letters, and tell her that you love her and that flying is not nearly as terrifying as her parents had said. Tell her parents that, in fact, you did find it terrifying but were trying to make your wife less worried.

Tell your two daughters they're beautiful and that you miss them and that you'll be gone only for a little while. Tell them that when you get home you'll take them searching for horny toads. Then hang up and cry.

Cry as hard as you want, because no one can see you. Don't make a habit of it though, you need to be strong. Pray to God. Ask him for forgiveness, but also ask him for strength. Pray for luck and for happiness, and pray that soon you'll be able to return home. Pray that everything will work out. Then, find a Christian church nearby and familiarize yourself with it. It will be important in the future.

Finally, prepare for your interview. Make sure your hair is braided, your jeans and shirt unwrinkled, and don't wear your hat, even though you love it. City men find hats in the workplace disrespectful. They don't understand your cultural identity, and they won't try to. Don't try to make them.

During the interview, reiterate that you're from Dulce, New Mexico. It's better than saying you came from a reservation. City men will think you're lazy. They don't like reservations, and they don't understand them. They won't realize that you, too, are American. And never forget that either: You are an American.

Make it clear that English is your first language. When they notice that you also speak Athabaskan, they're going to come to their own conclusions. Let them, but enunciate your words clearly. If you think it will help, practice on getting rid of your slight accent, but you need to practice this well in advance, because you don't want to slip. You'll be nervous, but breathe, be friendly, be conversational. Be yourself.

Don't become angry if the interviewer asks if you drink. Maybe he asks everyone that question during interviews. Or maybe the company has a very strict policy about alcohol consumption. Maybe the interviewer simply wants to know if you'd be interested later that evening in joining him at a bar.

Once you do land a job, be careful with your money. Understand how much you have and how to spend it. Buy only the necessities—food, rent, deodorant, shampoo. Everything else is unnecessary. Remember that you're trying to provide for your family, not just yourself. Set aside a certain amount every month for your family back home, and be proud of it. Even a few dollars is more than what you were making. Your family will be proud, your wife will boast about you to neighbors.

On Sundays, go to church. At church, be courteous. Impress those attending with your knowledge of scripture, and be as active as you can. Volunteer for the Easter food drive, socialize, smile, be happy to be there. Tell anyone who asks that you come from New Mexico. Even in church, where your mind should be free to express itself, people will judge you. Realize that's how city men are.

As the months go by, you may forget the three dimples that make a triangle on the side of your oldest daughter's forehead. You may forget that when your youngest daughter hugged you, the top of her head came to your waist. Ask for pictures, as many as your wife and her parents can send. Smile when you see their face again, and gaze in amazement at how old the two are getting. Call home to apologize to your eldest daughter for missing Keesta, but tell her you saw the pictures and that she looks beautiful. After she's finished crying, tell her about horny toads, then lie to her and say you'll be home soon. You may not realize it's a lie at the time. You also think you'll be home soon. Tell your wife you love her, and tell her parents you love them, and tell your children that you love them even more. Hang up and cry.

Stay strong. You'll spend so much time denying who you are and where you're from that you'll begin believing you're someone else. Call your wife and ask her to send some of the baskets she makes so you can put them around the apartment. Dig that favorite hat of yours out from the neglected bottom drawer and wear it around town when you're off work. As you walk around the city, you can look, but don't buy. Maybe purchase a small souvenir for your wife—a pair of fifty-dollar earrings. But otherwise keep to the necessities.

When September rolls around, your wife will call you to remind you about Go-Jii-Yah. Apologize for forgetting and send the earrings you bought her through the mail. They'll arrive too late for her to wear during the feast, but she'll get them. When she does, she'll call you and thank you and tell you how much she loves you and how badly she wants you to come home. You two will talk for hours. Don't use slang you picked up in the city, because she'll ask you what it means and then tell you not to use it again.

A year will pass, and your boss will tell you he wants to give you a raise. He'll tell you he was impressed and surprised by your hard work. Thank him. Disregard his use of the word "surprised."

Fly home to celebrate. When you arrive, you'll feel out of place. Hug your daughters—the youngest one's head will reach past your belly button. See your wife wearing the earrings you bought her and kiss her. Allow her parents to welcome you home with their delicious fry bread. The fry bread you almost forgot existed. Tell your family about the city and how different it is, but leave out the bad parts. Don't tell them about the looks you get when you get on the bus in the morning, or the reaction coworkers have when they see your long hair.

Your wife's parents will tell you about an opening for a job at the casino and will ask you to take it. Tell them about your raise, and tell them you'd make more than twice the amount in the city than at the casino. Her parents will be saddened by the news, but they won't press further. Your wife will also be disheartened, so you'll squeeze her arm and kiss her like you used to when you were younger and more optimistic.

When the family is done with dinner, take your two daughters on a hike in the sagebrush and catch a horny toad. Tell them how the animals used to be common, until they were driven away and killed. They'll hold the animal and run their fingers down its prickly back and giggle. Then take them to the general store and buy them ice cream. They'll laugh and giggle some more and tell you how much they missed you. You'll walk by neighbors on your way home and some will address you in Athabaskan. You'll take a moment to respond.

Spend a week with your family and learn all the things you missed during the year. See even more pictures of your daughters and wife. Then, your time will be up. Go to the small Dulce airport and leave for the city. When you arrive, tell the taxi where to go, and the driver will welcome you home.

Smile. The increased income will be relieving. Start picturing your daughters going to college, graduating, and becoming doctors. Life will be looking up, but don't let it get to your head. You'll consider moving your whole family to the city but realize that's impossible. Instead, work harder than ever. When you walk around town, still wear your hat. Your excuse will be that it no longer fits, but arrogance does not actually lead to a big head. Decide to buy a used truck so you won't have to take the city bus to work. With your purchase comes car insurance and more money will get taken from your monthly paycheck. But buy one because everyone else has a car, and on

Sundays drive yourself to church and pray for your family and for the friends you've made in the city.

When September comes, you'll remember Go-Jii-Yah. Call your wife. Hear bad news. Take a vacation day and visit your oldest daughter. Don't fly, drive: her medicine is expensive. Go back to the city to pay for it. You'll want to be with her, but without the medication she might not make it.

For another two months, work harder than any other man in the company. Take extra hours, stop spending money on lunches, and only rest during church. Hang a picture of her above the altar so your church can pray for your daughter. Call her every night to hear her voice. Tell her her favorite tale about Raven and Coyote. When she cries and asks you to come home, tell her everything will be alright.

***

Return home for the funeral. Decide on a Christian burial. Look at her face for the last time before she's lowered into the earth. Spot her three dimples and then notice a fourth. Realize how much of her life you missed. Your wife will cry, but you'll cry harder. The oaths will be spoken in Athabaskan, and you'll have a hard time following some of it. When the funeral ends, don't let your first thought be to move back to the city for work. If you share this with your wife, she'll lock herself in the bathroom and refuse to come out.

If you take your now oldest daughter on a hike, there will be no laughing. Instead of horny toads, you'll see snakes.

Your boss will call to tell you a new position in the company has opened up, and it pays twice as much as the one you have. Tell him what happened. He'll tell you he's sorry and to call him back when you're finished mourning. Your wife's parents will overhear the conversation and again point to the job at the casino. Tell them it isn't enough pay.

Cut your hair short and return to the city. Get the new position and the raise. When you call your wife, she'll barely talk. Your daughter will be the same. When she does talk, she'll ask only one question. Respond the same every time: "Yes, I will be there for your Keesta. And no, I won't miss it." When you go to church, take your daughter's picture down. The other families may offer you condolences, but ask them to pray for your family instead.

A night will come when you wake up in the darkness and wonder where you are. Ask yourself why you went back to the city. Ask yourself why you left your family behind. Don't justify everything with the number on your paycheck. Your work will suffer, and you'll finally have a meeting with your boss. He'll tell you he's happy you're back, but not happy about your performance. Tell him more than he should know about your family troubles. He'll offer to pay to move your family to the city. He'll tell you money can solve your problem. Seriously consider the option, and tell him you'll ask your wife.

As you leave, he'll see your hair and say that you've finally become a city man. He'll say he's glad to see a born- and-bred Native American embrace American culture. Don't tell him that you cut your hair in mourning. He'd never understand.

Realize no city man would ever understand why you cut your hair. Remember the shame as you cut away at the locks you had been so proud to wear. Remember your daughter and the three dimples on her forehead. Remember the one dimple that you'd never met because you were never around.

Tell him you are American and always have been.

Quit your job and move back home. Your daughter will hug you, and your wife will kiss you, and her parents will welcome you home with fry bread. There will be no laughter, but you will all be a family again. Fill out an application for the job at the casino. Get it and start work. Get rid of your truck to pay for your daughter's Keesta, and during her ceremony sit by your wife and her parents. For the first time in months, smile. Smile so broad your cheeks touch the brim of your favorite hat. Finally, turn to your wife and tell her that you have never been more proud to be a Jicarilla Apache.

Tomorrowland Today

ELIZABETH ENGEL, Grade 12, Age 17. Mamaroneck High School,
Mamaroneck, NY, James Short, *Educator*

Sometimes PJ wonders why she has freckles. Today isn't such
a day—the wind is stronger than it really should be in Florida,
even if it is November, and the smell of creosote and exhaust
isn't something anyone should really be forced to endure for
more than twenty minutes straight. Unfortunately, Disney
World has not yet received that memo, and so here she is, stuck
at the Tomorrowland Speedway for another hour.

It wouldn't be so bad if it weren't for the smell. The job itself
is pretty mechanical. All she has to do is raise her fingers and
tell the riders which station to park at: 1, 2, 3, 4, 5, 6, and then
over and over again. It doesn't require much thought at all,
and in that regard, PJ likes working the speedway; it wouldn't
be bad; not at all, if it wasn't for the smell. It gives PJ time to
think, usually stupid things like why she has freckles when no
one else in her family does, or why her brother is marrying
Tracy, of all people. Tracy.

But today PJ is thinking, *I hate Shira*. Today she's thinking,
*I hate Shira, and I don't want to, but I hate her so much and I
wish I didn't but I do, I do.* And she's thinking of Shira's plaited
hair and Shira's gold earrings and Shira, and Shira, and Shira,

God, she hates Shira. Shira's smile when she backed PJ against a wall and whispered that she won. Shira's smile when she knew she had Max. 1, 2, 3, 4, 5, 6, 1, 2, 3, 4, 5, 6, and still every thought goes back to Shira.

I'm so glad I'm working Tomorrowland today, Anna thinks, looking over at PJ and her combat boots, the way they skid on the racetrack, and then she reverses her train of thought, and wonders about the phrase Tomorrowland today, wonders about PJ, wonders about the night they had gotten drunk together and PJ had said, "I hate my job, I hate it so much," only after taking three shots, and Anna had wanted to say, I wish you loved it. I wish I could make you love it. I wish I could be the reason you love it. Instead she said, "Well, look on the bright side: at least we're not working Animal Kingdom." And PJ had laughed, and that was almost as good. Almost.

Almost almost almost. The word, she thinks, sounds like someone hesitating. All, says the man in her mind, and then amends, most. Anna hears the sound of two of the metal bumpers on the car bumping into each other, harder than usual, and turns to look at what caused the noise, only to be met with the sight of what looks like a five-year-old boy who had somehow hooked one of his tires over the metal boundary.

"Ugh," PJ mutters, and walks toward the car after rolling her eyes at Anna, and the boy in car seven watches her go and thinks, *Those are the boots Susie had, I'm sure of it, I'm sure they're still in my closet, just like that dress she wore to Hannah's party, just like her pajamas, just like the Yale shirt she bought when she visited her brother, two sizes too big, the way it fit like an avalanche, the way my name sounded whenever she was wearing slippers, the way she said Aaron, and it didn't sound like a name, it sounded like a prayer.* He inches his car forward, not looking at the track, looking at the boots, and PJ was fixing the car and thinking, *I know what it's like to be jealous. I know it in my veins, what it's like to hold a person next to you like you hold blood in the veins and then to hold a person not at all. I know it, my iliac bone knows it, knows what it's like to support empty space. I know this, I wish I didn't but I know this, and I hate Shira so much. I've never hated anyone so quickly except Hadley, and I only hated her because Max did. I would've hated anyone for him, even then.*

PJ walks toward Anna again after the car is back on track, and Aaron thinks, *Susie,* and Anna thinks of the line of poetry that PJ has tattooed on her arm, that she had only seen bits and pieces of until two weeks ago, when they had gotten drunk together, thinks about the other thing, the relentless thing, your body drowning in gravity. When Anna had asked her about it, PJ shut down, not drunk enough, she said, I'm just not drunk enough. And Anna could hear the defeat in her voice. Anna could hear it.

Anna thinks about what it would be like to drown in gravity. Anna thinks about how she already is, thinks about Tomorrowland today. She wonders what PJ would think if she said it out loud.

She looks over as PJ's hands form a perfect five, palm spread out, lifeline vulnerable, and says, "Have you ever considered that every day we work in Tomorrowland, it's today in Tomorrowland? Tomorrowland today." And PJ smiles, says, "Irony's a bitch," putting another finger up to tell the next driver to go to slot six. Anna thinks that PJ's pointer finger is perfect. The driver follows, gives her an obvious once over. If she weren't at Disney right now, PJ would've flipped him off, said "Go to hell," but she is at Disney. She's stuck at Disney. She should be stuck with Max. She's stuck in this Tomorrowland uniform on this stupid track, and creosote is stuck in her nostrils, and none of it is okay, and she wishes that she were anywhere else but To-morrowland today. And PJ thinks, *I would've carved up ground for you. I would've planted millions of gardens for you*, thinks, *I hate Shira*. Thinks, *please, please, get me out of Tomorrowland today. I'd do anything to get out of Tomorrowland today.*

How to Become Yourself

HOLLY CHEN, Grade 9, Age 14. Carlmont High School, Belmont, CA,
Jody Humes, *Educator*

You're eight years old, squinting like Clint Eastwood under the summer sun, and wish you were with your mom at the spa, watching her get pedicures, and maybe later she would let you get one too. You hear your dad say, "Son, eyes on the ball," but when you turn, the mud-speckled ball hurtles itself toward you. You jump to the side and let it pass. "Son, why'd you do that?" You hear your father. "Because it's dirty!" He puts his hands together and squeezes them across his forehead and sighs like a deflating balloon. You see the disappointment on everyone's faces and walk off the field with hot eyes. You wish you were Clint Eastwood so you could just roam around the desert catching bandits, brave and winning all the time.

There's a boy in high school with thick eyelashes, a buzz cut, and muscled arms. His name is Cliff. He's one of the few who talks to you and always asks what you think about girls' butts. You always reply, "Looks like a butt to me." Cliff thinks you're funny. You often find yourself staring at him even though he is dating Lainey, the petite dance captain. Partly because of your father's pressure, you join the football team, but as a sweet bonus, Cliff is there. You're a bench warmer on the team. Though you trip a lot and bruise like an apple during games and practice, Cliff doesn't notice you in the way you want him to. On the last day of graduation, while streamers fly and litter the ground, and you know some poor janitor is going to have to spend the whole night cleaning it, you walk up to Cliff. He gives you a big bear hug and says, "I can't believe we're graduating, man." But you say, "I like you." You feel your cheeks go on fire, like the engines to a rocket. He looks at you, and his eyebrows slowly knit together, while his mouth curls to a slow frown, and he says disgustedly, "Don't be a fag, man."

During college, a pretty brown-haired girl named Janie follows you around. She is in many of your classes and has a heart as big as the Eiffel Tower. One day, after class, she brings you to a corner in the hallway and kisses you. "I love you," she says, with her brown eyes staring into yours, covering you like a warm blanket. You try to tell her the truth, but then that voice and word start to repeat in your head. So when you open your mouth, the words come out different: "I love you too." After half a year of dating, she bugs you to take her to your parents. Your father nods as if she's a brand new Ferrari, your brother claps your back and gives you a knowing wink, while your little sister adores Janie and makes her a macaroni necklace. Only your mother seems unhappy, and before dinner, she excuses herself to her room.

After returning to school, your relationship with Janie feels no longer like a warm blanket protecting you. Instead it feels like a noose tied around your neck, and every day it gets tighter. She doesn't know the words that she considers harmless and innocent suffocate the most. Eventually, you try to break up with her. "I'm sorry," are the words that fill and linger in the air. At first she cries and blames herself, asking if it was her who did something wrong. You want to tell her it isn't her that is wrong; it's you. The truth tries to burst out of your mouth, like a frog trying to leap out of a cage. But all you can do is stand there, something part of the scenery, a detached statue. She sees how emotionless you are, an impassive stranger to a troublesome five-year-old. She quiets her cries, and with her back hunched under her red coat, she walks away, her red scarf flying in the air, standing out from the snow surrounding you and her. That's the last time you see her.

The phone rings as you groggily reach to answer it. Life has been on hold. Out of shame, you've stopped going to school, fearing you'll see Janie, and feel those pangs of pain. Your mother calls. "Sweetheart, what's wrong? You haven't called for days." You reply, "I feel guilty about Janie, like I've robbed months from her that she could've spent with some guy who really loved her. It is all because of . . ." You hear a smile through the phone, as she says, "I've known for a long time what kind of life you've been living. Eventually, you have to stop running away from yourself. Now let your freak flag fly and embrace yourself."

You've returned to school. On campus, you bump into this boy. He's very tall, African-American, and speaks like a bubbling river. He has blue-tipped dreadlocks and wears old clothes covered in paint. You always invite him to coffee, and the two of you sit there at a table; he draws while you sip a double-shot caramel espresso while staring at him. He never once looks up from drawing to talk to you, but for some reason, you like it this way. Two people just enjoying one another's company. One day, all of a sudden, he looks up from drawing and hands you a thick manila envelope. Then he abruptly picks up his bags and walks out of the coffee shop. Inside you find a comic titled "Fighting for Love, the Tale of Me and You." Little sobs of pure laughter escape your body, as a silent, giddy Yes escapes you.

You stay in New York with the boy with dreadlocks. You call him "Joe-Joe" because of the pleasurable sound of that nickname, and also because he likes to eat sloppy Joes. Walking in a park, hand in hand, wrapped in a scarf is how you spend time together. He is your quiet supporter; never once has he judged you for trying to keep your relationship a secret. He understands how hard it is for you even now, and he accepts you. When days are stressful and all you want to do is curl into a ball and watch hours of *Modern Family*, he is the one covering a blanket over you and popping popcorn. He stays up long late hours, with jazz music oozing out of his studio. You watch as his brows furrow, when his hands create short, frisk moves of passion that breathe life into a blank slate. He chases his dreams, dreams that he longs to paint, paint on his canvas of life.

One day, your father is on a business trip to learn how the branch in New York manages new accounting recruits. He decides to surprise you by paying you a visit. Your boyfriend opens the door wearing a holey T-shirt with dried paint and baggy sweatpants from his old high school. Your dad looks up at him as if he is a rare African giraffe and says, "I must've come to the wrong apartment." You appear, hugging your boyfriend from behind before you realize your father is at your door. You drop your arms to your sides and freeze. Slowly you open your mouth to say, "I have something to tell you, Dad. Why don't you come in?" For a moment, your father's face looks like he just ate something sour. Then it returns to the blank slate it usually is. Your father walks away as if he really did just knock on some stranger's door and doesn't even cast you a sideways glance. You feel even smaller compared to him, an ant compared to a redwood tree. You finally realize that you will never be the son he wanted, and that the only person you can ever be is you.

Your brother calls you the next day to say that your parents are fighting. He says, "Dad wants to disown you because he saw you with some man, hugging. He must be getting old and seeing things! He thinks you're gay," he scoffs, "and Mom says if he disowns you, she'll divorce him." Your brother sounds like a skeptic. "But I am gay," you reply, feeling disconnected from space and time, and your brother goes silent before the line goes dead.

A few weeks later, your mother phones to say that she is getting a divorce. You drive to your old home to bring her to the airport. She is standing outside, with the wind blowing against her face, bouncing her springy brown hair back and forth. She wears a soft-pink billowy sundress, and in her hands she carries an old red suitcase. She smiles at you and runs to give you a hug so warm it could make a freezer melt. She feels as light as a balloon, as though she is going to float away.

During the drive, she smiles and says, "I'm going to Africa to explore the jungle. I always wanted to go there, even on my honeymoon, but instead we went shopping in France. I want to do things I like instead of doing everything your father likes." The more she rambles on about how she is going on vacation, the more her wrinkles seem to disappear. Years of worry seem to fall off her face, leaving her lighter and lighter, till she flies away, all the way to Africa.

One day, at the same coffee shop that you and Dangelo spent hours in, Dangelo asks you to marry him. Dangelo looks up at you, and when you look into his eyes, your heart explodes. Emotions cascade out of you like a waterfall, and your voice leaps with happiness as you utter that definitive "Yes."

You are unsure about inviting your father and siblings to the wedding. "They had never accepted you in the beginning. Why ask them now?" your boyfriend asks while making frittatas one Sunday morning. But in your heart, you know things cannot be left the way they are now. You call your father, but he doesn't answer, so you leave a message. Then you call your brother and sister. They say things like, "Maybe. We're kind of busy." You ask about your father, and they say, "He doesn't want to talk to you."

On your wedding day, you go to town hall, and you're surprised to see that your brother and sister have come. Your brother grabs you into a hug, saying, "I was wrong. To even believe that I would stop loving the brother I have loved all my life, just because he's gay is . . ." You look up at him and see the love in his eyes, and finish his sentence for him. "Incredibly stupid," you say. "I just can't believe you'd be dumb enough to do that." He laughs as he pulls you into a tight hug. Your sister creeps behind you two, wrapping her arms around you all like a protective layer. Your siblings are only smiles as they continue life with you in it.

As years roll by, every Christmas a gift is delivered to your house, without the sender's name on it. And every year it is the same thing, a bottle of Cakebread wine. Last Christmas, your brother calls you and tells you to come to the hospital. When you arrive, you see your father on the white hospital bed, wrapped in a baggy cloth. He seems washed out, resembling the sickly white color of the walls, bed, and everything else in that room. As he rests in his bed, his milky eyes wander upon you. Instantly they open wide, and you see something awake inside him. You reach to grab his withered hand that shakes. Sighing, he looks at you, and whispers, "Are you happy?" When you nod, he closes his eyes and falls asleep, only he never wakes again. Ever since then, you haven't received a bottle of Cakebread.

You now live in a townhouse with a little girl whom you have adopted and a loving husband. It is the most blissful of times. The pride that swells inside when that rainbow flag pin is worn makes you feel strong. It seems you have finally become yourself. Strength gave you love and love gave you happiness.

The Harvard Hopeful's Handbook

CAROLYN KELLY, Grade 12, Age 17. Glenbrook South High School, Glenview, IL, Cheryl Hope, *Educator*

Sander Prescott stared aghast at the book lying in wait for him on his desk (aghast: adj, struck with overwhelming shock or amazement; filled with sudden fright or horror; "lying," not "laying," when an object is resting somewhere). Another prep book?

But this one had neither the glossy cover nor the monstrous width of your typical ACT/SAT/AP bible. *The Harvard Hopeful's Handbook* was printed in small gold type on a crimson hardback cover, and the spine was thinner than two No. 2 pencils stacked together. It wasn't in the pristine condition he usually received his books in, either—no secondhand, eraser-smudged practice texts for Sander Prescott. Yet this book was well worn: corners thumbed down, binding frayed, cover discolored. There was no note of explanation.

Unusual condition aside, Sander knew the routine: If there was a book, or a test, or an application lying on the desk when he returned home from school, he was to begin it as soon as he had finished the rest of his assignments for the day—or night, rather, as the work for his six advanced classes absorbed all daylight, even in the last long days of summer.

Sander sat down and moved the book aside to make room for the homework that would emerge as soon as he opened his backpack.

Pulled on the zipper and reached in.

Found his textbooks and notebooks by touch. Arranged them on the desk.

Began to consume daylight.

He sat motionless for a few minutes. Tried to blame it on inertia (physics: the property of matter by which it retains its state of rest or its velocity along a straight line so long as it is not acted upon by an external force). Finally got up, closed the blinds, and opened his backpack.

At 8 o'clock, his parents came home. They ate at 9 o'clock, to give his mother time to cook the homemade meal that would give him the edge in his scores.

Before Sander had been born, he had been Sandra, according to the ultrasounds. His parents had been thrilled, because schools had to admit more girls back then. Today they point to the statistics that say that women now have the majority in enrollment (58 percent of those enrolled in two- and four-year colleges), and how fortunate that he should be applying just as schools are being pressured to accept more men.

They despair a little that colleges want so much international diversity, but are bolstered by the hope that applying from the Midwest is more original than following the East Coast boarding school track.

Sander suspects that the reason that they don't have more parent friends is that their conversations have always started like this:

"Has [child of Sander's age] thought about college yet?" Since third grade.

During dinner, Sander asked his parents about the book. His mother explained that a colleague at work had heard—like all the other parents had "heard," surely—about Sander's aspirations (n, strong desire, longing, or aim; ambition) and had passed on the handbook that had gotten his niece, his niece's former best friend's boyfriend, and the boyfriend's twin brother into Harvard. It had been circulating among the ambitious for years, the colleague said, though he had never heard exactly what it was about.

"It couldn't hurt," his father said, and blew on a forkful of organic mac and cheese.

Sander was excused from doing the dishes because he had the new book to cogitate (v, to think deeply about; ponder). Back in his bedroom, he ran through a last set of flash cards for the biology quiz tomorrow, then pulled out a highlighter and sticky notes. Time to attack the book. Before he could begin, his mother knocked on his door.

Sander said nothing. By saying goodnight at 10:30 every night, his parents liked to imagine their son going to bed and sleeping the eight hours prescribed for a healthy teenager. It was a charade on all sides, because he knew that they knew that in order to maintain the grades and the test scores they needed from him, he couldn't afford to waste eight hours on sleep. The healthy sleep standard was an exception for Sander, reserved for test days only.

When he could no longer hear her lingering outside his room, he flipped open the book. He peeled the dedication page (To my son) away from the first page and began to read.

"Dear Hopeful, Good evening.

How do we know that you are reading this during the evening hours?

Because we have been there, in those solitary nights where

the desk lamp works sunset through sunrise. We know that to contend for the most prestigious, the most iconic, the most illustrious university in the world, you have been toiling all day on the APs, the student council, the debate team, volunteering and now, the applications.

We have been there. And now we are here: esteemed alums, grateful for all the opportunities that Harvard has bestowed us and keen to give back. We're going to commence with you.

Why?

Because you work harder than the desk lamp. Because you possess the drive and the ambition for a school with the best reputation in the world. Because you hunger for this so badly that everybody knows it—that is how this handbook arrived on your desk.

Hopeful, the path that you are about to embark upon will not be easy. Our instructions will push you to the very edge of your impressive ability. But we vow, Hopeful, that all strife will be forgotten when you read that glorious acceptance, when you pull on that crimson jacket, and when you see that Cambridge is where you belong.

VERITAS."

Sander leaned back in his chair in a manner that could possibly be taken as a slouch. It was dark outside, and his parents were asleep. He thought about making some coffee.

We have been there, in those solitary nights where the desk lamp works sunset through sunrise. A lamp is to daylight as ambition is to dreams.

And now we are here: esteemed alums . . .

A lamp is to daylight as esteem is to respect. A lamp is to daylight as Hopeful is to Sander.

He didn't make any coffee, but crawled into bed without setting an alarm.

The next morning, he woke up to daylight. It was 8:23 and first period was nearly halfway over. He opened all his blinds and went back to sleep. He was awakened some time later by the shrill ringing of the telephone. Distantly he heard the voicemail pick it up, and the recorded voice enlightening the kitchen that Sand-er Pres-cott had been marked absent in first, second, and third periods on Friday, August 30.

Sander did not feel panicked. He did not feel rebellious, either. He did feel slightly dazed, reacclimating (v, to become readjusted) to sleep and sunlight. With the radiant day assaulting his exposed windows, he considered his options.

Sander Prescott has been marked absent in three periods today. Sander should:

Get dressed and hurry to school.

Pretend to be his father and call to excuse himself from the rest of the day, dental emergency.

Run away to live on his grandparents' dairy farm.

None of the above.

Sander knew how to take tests. He scored in the 99th percentile of all ACT/SAT/AP takers because he could identify the right choice with little deliberation. Hours of prep and tutoring had drilled into him the strategies and the patterns and the rational process of selecting the best answer—yet nowhere had he been told to nurture his instincts, to prepare for the day where there is no formula for the right choice, though in the arena of life there rarely is.

According to all the tactics he applied, plans A or B were the best. If he returned to class now, he would minimize the loss of instruction as well as the amount of make-up work. If he feigned an emergency, he could take the full day off with no repercussions for his attendance. His parents could understand oversleeping or needing a day of recovery in senior year.

Nothing would change.

Sander stared out the window until the glare filled his vision. He could no longer see his desk, his backpack, his bookshelf. Choose the best answer.

Cambridge is where you belong.

His parents left in the dark and came back in the dark. Nothing would change.

He didn't want to answer the same questions. He didn't want to follow a handbook, didn't want his responsibilities laid out for him on a desk.

This was the VERITAS: Sander wanted to choose "None of the above." He wanted to embark upon a path with no idea of what lay at the end. He wanted to have a conversation with his parents about their favorite jokes or their first car accidents. He wanted to join a club that wouldn't impress anybody at all on his application. He wanted to write a story without a word limit.

He wasn't sure what any of this meant for his future. His momentum up to this point had been so great that he was afraid slamming the brakes now would completely derail the Prescotts. Better to gradually lower the acceleration until the motion simply ceased. His parents could come to see that a reversal today was better than one a year or two in the future, after they had dropped astronomical sums into tuition and dropped his attendance into every conversation.

Yes, he would formulate these arguments, begin to plan anew, because if he was going to make his own choices, he wanted them to be right. But not yet—not today. He deserved to spend one entire day finding out what he liked without the shadow of the future darkening his daylight.

Resolved, Sander blinked his stinging eyes and leapt out of bed, banging his toes in the rush before his vision cleared.

There was no time to waste. He would take the day's unexcused absence without worrying about how it would appear on his record, but he would make it count.

For breakfast, he ordered to-go from the family-owned pancake house and picked it up in his pajamas. He sat outside on his back porch and tried to eat it all, but could manage only half.

He created a Facebook account and had made 20 friends before he logged off. Clearly, other teenagers didn't actually study during study hall.

When he would have been in AP Biology, he soaked in the hot tub his parents never used, and he thought for a long time.

After school would have gotten out, he retrieved the pathetically deflated basketball from under the back porch and pumped it back to health. He had played intramural hoops for the first two years of high school but had stopped when he became too tired.

Later he called his friends for homework, but only for the classes he really cared about.

When his parents came home at 8 o'clock, he was lying on the couch, eating the leftover pancakes and watching *The Hangover*, which he had never seen before. Who comes up with this stuff, he was thinking. How does your story become something that people let into their lives?

Maanvaasani

CARA MAINES, Grade 10, Age 16. St. John's Upper School, Houston, TX, Brian Beard, *Educator*

Undaana kaayam yaavum thannaaalae aari poagum. Maayam enna ponmaanae, ponmaanae. Enna kaayam anna podhum.
The wounds inflicted on me will heal by themselves. There's no mystery in that, my love, my love. I will be able to stand.
—Traditional Tamil lullaby

I.
"Maayam enna ponmaanae ponmaanae," Nadiya sings. The storm has stopped, but Nadiya's window is still shrouded by a faint mist of rainwater. Nadiya smiles as she tucks a strand of dark hair into her thick braid. It is not quite yet daybreak, so the haze of the inky sky masks the thin layer of white paint peeling off the wall. She can just make out the profile of her daughter's cradle in the corner of the kitchen.

Nadiya uses a fork and bowl in place of a mortar and pestle to grind together black lentils and short-grain rice on the kitchen counter. In her homeland of Sri Lanka, Nadiya would mix her long, flaky rice with lentils, mustard seeds, ginger root, and chili peppers so spicy they made her mouth numb. Then she would fill her batter with coconut filling and pour it into pans for her pressure cooker.

In America, things are different. Instead of her mustard seeds, Nadiya uses packets of mustard she finds in the super-market's 99-cent aisle. In place of the tangy coconut filling she readily found back home, she must use the saccharine coconut flakes from the baking section. And to Nadiya's greatest dis-may, she must make do with bland, watery "hot" sauce instead of zesty chili peppers. At the closest supermarket, the only spicy food Nadiya can find is from the "foreign foods" aisle, where matzo and cups of Ramen sit next to soggy jarred curry and prepackaged taco shells.

Nadiya spoons the batter for these cakes, *idli*, into her pan and stares out the window. "Enna kaayam anna podhum," she sings to her daughter in lilting Tamil. The infant's name is Aabarna, but Nadiya knows that when Aabarna enters grade school, she will be called Abby. The other mothers in the building have explained this to her. In America, names are important, they say. In America, a person must have the right name to be treated the right way. This is a new generation, Nadiya has learned, a generation of Midhurnas turned Mias, Saanvis turned Saras.

Nadiya caresses the soft wisps of black hair on Aabarna's head, staring into the infant's copper eyes as she sings the next verse of the lullaby, "yen maeni thangi kollum." As each word flutters across her tongue, she hears her mother's words echoed in her own.

II.

In Sri Lanka, the earth was softer, gentler. Nadiya could walk outside without shoes, and the ground beneath her felt like it was holding a secret. There was a quiet energy radiating from the land; her feet connected to the deep, rich dirt. In America, at least where she has been, there is only pavement, cracked and split, with weeds sprouting between the broken fragments of concrete.

Nadiya spent most mornings before primary school sitting at the table in their small kitchen, watching her mother, Maathasi, cook breakfast. She and her brother Ghanan played hand games. They were still at an age when Nadiya wore her ebony hair in shiny plaits and Ghanan built model train sets. Maathasi sang songs every morning as they drank warm milk and ate slices of ripe banana, usually playful songs like "Laali, Laali," but sometimes more somber songs like "Undaana Kaayam."

Nadiya asked her mother about the lullaby once, when she was nine and Ghanan was twelve. "Why do you sing 'Undaana Kaayam' to children?" she wondered. "It's so sad, Amma."

"Come help me, Nadiya," she said to the girl, who sat at the table threading a pink ribbon through her braids. Maathasi molded balls of lentils and rice for idli. "Undaana Kaayam is a song about two people in love," she said.

"I know that, Amma," Nadiya sighed. "But why is it so sad? If they love each other, why is there talk of wounds and pain?"

"Sometimes, Nadiya, when you love someone so much, you have to lie to them," her mother said. "When you love someone, you will be hurt in ways neither of you understand, in ways you've never felt before. Sometimes you just can't tell the person you love, because you love them too much to let them feel your pain."

"Have you ever done that, Amma?" Nadiya asked.

Maathasi did not reply to this question. Fingers trembling ever so slightly, she delicately and deliberately flattened the lentil-rice balls into cakes. She stared out the window, where it had just begun to rain, and pulled her daughter closer.

III.

After leaving her own daughter with the next-door neighbor, Nadiya walks to the bus stop. She makes sure to be careful where she steps, so that the shards of beer bottles and chewed gum on the sidewalk do not blemish her shoes. When she reaches the bus stop, the bus has not arrived, so she must sit on the bench, stare at her shoes, and wait.

Nadiya loves this feeling, the atmosphere the earth takes on just after it rains. It reminds her of a memory she can't quite place, of new beginnings and fresh starts and all the other clichés America once meant to her.

In Tamil, there is a word for this. It is *maanvaasani*, and it cannot be translated directly into English. Roughly, maanvaasani means the smell of the earth after it has rained. In America, maanvaasani is a little damper, duller, dingier. Once the rain has subsided, the moisture lingers in the air and traps the scents of cigarettes and car exhaust. It does not fill with the smell of rice pudding with almonds and cardamom, nor the haunting perfume of cut orchids that she remembers from the markets in her hometown of Colombo.

There are more things Nadiya cannot translate, besides maanvaasani. She cannot translate the lack of belonging she feels, the ties that have frayed, the passage of time. She cannot translate the moment she saw her father fall to his knees at the sight of his son's corpse; the lonely flower perched above her father's grave.

Nadiya is beginning to think that maybe even less can be translated into words, English or Tamil, than she thought. The bus arrives, and she steps on.

IV.

When Nadiya stepped into the airport of Colombo for the first time, she was fixated on details that no one else seemed to notice: the acerbic smell of cleaning fluid that pervaded the waiting rooms; the mismatched, slightly crooked tiles on the floor; the askew nametag of the man who checked her in. The airport was a menacing place, a chilling contrast to her sunny neighborhood, and there was something not quite right about everything. Nadiya hoped that this did not subtly foreshadow what was to come.

Nadiya was nineteen years old, armed with only her flimsy suitcase and a Tamil-English dictionary, accompanied by her mother, Maathasi.

Maathasi braided Nadiya's hair that morning, for the first time in over five years. "You want to make a good impression," she told Nadiya, but Nadiya could guess her mother's real intentions. The ritual was subdued, yet there was almost an unspoken tension in the realization that this was the last time and in the knowledge that both of the women were holding back tears. There should be a word for the last time your mother braids your hair, thought Nadiya.

At the airport, though, Maathasi exuded calm energy, a quiet acceptance. As it neared time for Nadiya to board her plane, Maathasi put her hands on her daughter's shoulders.

"When you land at the airport in Chicago, look for your Uncle Prashnev. He'll take care of you," she said.

"I know, Amma," sighed Nadiya. "You've told me a million times."

"Don't forget to go to temple, Nadiya."

"Amma, it's almost time. I know," Nadiya said.

Maathasi stared straight into Nadiya's eyes this time. "I'm doing this because I love you," she said, sounding as if she had almost convinced herself. "You know you'll have a better life. I want a spotless future for you. You deserve opportunities. You deserve better than this. You don't want your children to grow up here."

Nadiya smiled halfheartedly. "I know."

Maathasi glanced down at the crooked tiles, her hands still perched on Nadiya's shoulders. Though her posture was confident, her eyes, glistening amber, betrayed her.

"I love you, Amma," Nadiya said, trying to sound confident. "We'll talk on the telephone soon. We'll write thousands of letters. One day you can come visit."

Nadiya could have sworn that as she walked away, she heard someone faintly humming "Undaana Kaayam."

V.

Nadiya approaches the white brick house with the same trepidation she always does. It reminds her of a fortress, protected by thorny rose bushes and gated by a black fence. She uses her own key to unlock the door.

The woman pronounces her name jarringly, over-enunciating the i. "Nadiya, Katherine's sleeping," she says. "I'm about to leave for work. It would be great if you could get some laundry done while Kat's still asleep."

"Of course, Mrs. Coleman," Nadiya says.

She leaves her handbag on the kitchen table and begins to ascend the stairs. "Oh, and Nadiya? One last thing."

Nadiya steps down. "Yes?"

"You wouldn't mind staying after, would you? Tom and I have a dinner party to go to. It will only be a couple of hours," she says.

Nadiya sighs. "Of course, Mrs. Coleman."

"You're a blessing."

Nadiya climbs the flight of stairs until she reaches the nursery. Stepping into the cloyingly pastel-pink room, she notices that the baby has woken up. Clear blue eyes stare up at her, while the infant's mouth quivers, threatening to sob. Nadiya strokes the child's damp curls carefully, as if she were a fragile China doll, and begins to sing "Maayam enna ponmaanae ponmaanae."

Nadiya peers through the French windows. The rain is pouring again.

EMMA TROY, *Self Portrait*, Grade 12, Age 17. Washington-Lee High School, Arlington, VA. Hiromi Isobe, *Educator*. 2014 Gold Medal

ABOUT THE AUTHORS

DALIA AHMED is a junior at Miami Arts Charter School. Her work has appeared in *Dog Eat Crow, Postscript Literary Journal,* and *Of Love and Dedication.* Dalia lives in Miami, FL, with a large Afro-Arab family, colorful headscarves, and many bowls of hummus and pita bread.

HADASSAH AMANI lives in Florida. She receives inspiration from everything: from her experiences in everyday life to the books she used to read as a child. She hopes to someday become a food critic and vows to continue writing.

PHILIP ANASTASSIOU writes because he cannot not write. His peak writing hours are (much to the dismay of his internal sleeping patterns) around three to four in the morning. He does not sleep very much at all.

EMELINE ATWOOD started writing in the second grade when her grandmother began reading aloud her own poems about being with her grandfather. In elementary school, she kept poetry journals, but took her first creative writing class in high school.

HANEL BAVEJA'S writing portfolio is her exploration of place, or location, in shaping our identities. She believes that being an artist is a lens through which to view the world and our place in it. In the fall, she will attend Harvard University.

TUHFA BEGUM is a feminist, writer, and student of life. She resides in New York City. Tuhfa is a third-year mentee at Girls Write Now. When she is not reading or writing, she can be found sipping tea and dreaming of a more just and equal world, on her windowsill.

MOLLY BREITBART is a senior at Edgemont High School and will soon be a freshman at Skidmore College. Also a recipient of the 2014 River Styx Founder's Award, Molly writes because as Charles Bukowski once said, "[If you] take a writer away from his typewriter, all you have left is the sickness that started him writing in the first place."

JACKSON BROOK is co-editor-in-chief of Palo Alto High School's *Verde* magazine. Journalism allows him to learn new things and engage in conversations with interesting people. If he is able to give the reader a new perspective on something, then he considers to have done his job as a writer.

To HOLLY CHEN, courage is saying what other people don't want to say, doing what other people don't want to do, not minding or caring what other people think, and being someone other people don't want to be. She feels lucky that she has family and friends who have always inspired her to write.

Along with poetry, ZOE CHENG also writes fiction, stage plays, and screenplays. She constantly draws inspiration for her work from the world around her, and admires the potential of language to inspire both catharsis and empathy. She wishes to pursue a career in screenwriting.

RYAN CHUNG lives in Manhasset, New York, and is an eighth grader. His inspirations are music, traveling, and reading. In the future, Ryan wants to be a journalist and lawyer, and influence his community, writing about law and world events.

GEORGE COUNTS has lived in Charleston, South Carolina, for 17 years. He attends the Charleston County School of the Arts. His writing comes from both a compulsion that is skeletal, and a need to preserve the things that are fragile and ephemeral: his family, his friends, his environment. Writing keeps him grounded.

NATHAN CUMMINGS wrote ninety percent of his portfolio in the hours after 1 a.m. For him, writing is a means of filling in the gaps of the imagination, as well as an outgrowth of the early need to dream up make-believe games and worlds. He will attend Harvard University in the fall.

SHANNON DANIELS thinks in poetry and has learned that everything has a rhythm: the rumble of the 6 train is a song; streetlamps flicker to an invisible tune; she turns idioms, reminders, and memories into verses. She has lived in New York City all her life but will be moving to California this fall to study literature at Stanford University.

SOPHIA DIGGS-GALLIGAN is from Washington, D.C. She is inspired to write by nature, random strangers, disastrous news events, and books, as well as her family, friends, and wonderful writing teacher.

NICHOLAS ELDER, raised in Starkville, Mississippi, is a Frankenstein-esque collage of mismatched body parts: feet of a traveler, stomach of a chef, hands of a craftsman, eye of a photographer, heart of a poet . . . and yet he wants to study genetics. He writes to help make sense of his experiences and to make sure he remembers them for later.

ELIZABETH ENGEL writes because people and their stories fascinate her, and especially how much their stories overlap without ever being the same. Most recently, her writing has concentrated on love and sexuality, and how these experiences are inherently defined by the people with whom we surround ourselves.

JUSTIN GAINSLEY attends the Blake School in Minnetonka, Minnesota. He likes to write because it is an easy way to share his feelings and ideas with other people.

As a child, SARAH GAMARD drew pictures in notebooks to tell stories. Now she uses imagery in place of stick figures, and is a recent graduate of the New Orleans Center for Creative Arts.

JONATHAN GELERNTER is a 17-year-old Jew from Woodbridge, Connecticut. He's taller than his brother, and his interests include gangster movies, Meyer Lansky, and *Breaking Bad*. He thinks he's pretty funny.

C. SOPHIA GEORGE lives in Indianapolis, Indiana. She wrote "Winter" because of the freezing temperatures that occurred in Indiana last winter. She is firmly convinced that becoming an adult will never cause her to stop writing.

AVA GOGA is a part-time poet and full-time dreamer residing in Reno, Nevada. Poetry is more than just a way to express herself; it's a concise way to explore a topic and influence the opinion of an audience. When she's not writing, she paints landscapes or participates in her school's ROTC program.

LILY GORDON is a ninth-grader at Bard High School Early College in Manhattan. In "The Thing About Apples," she wanted to write about the racial prejudice experienced within the same "out" group, where someone is hated for having characteristics of the "in" group, yet ends up feeling like they belong nowhere.

SPENCER GRAYSON lives in Seattle, Washington. Writing allows her to enter a world where she can express innermost thoughts and feelings without being embarrassed by saying them out loud. She wants to be a novelist or a journalist, and since she reads even more than she writes, she'd love to be an editor as well!

EMILY GREEN is a half-Japanese writer and student living in America, studying French, and writing in English. She has a hankering for language, culture, animals, comic books, hot cocoa, and video games. She is a senior at the Appomattox Regional Governor's School for the Arts and Technology, and her current life's ambition is to hug an African lion.

STEPHANIE GUO writes because it forces her to look for meaning in the mundane. She is obsessed with politics, current events, and Chinese history, all of which find ways to seep into her writing. Sometimes, Stephanie thinks she is a starfish; other times, she wonders if she is growing up too quickly.

NOA GUR-ARIE is a junior at Bethesda-Chevy Chase High School, just outside of Washington, D.C. She has lived in Moscow, Russia, and spent her sophomore year in Rabat, Morocco, with the State Department's Kennedy-Lugar YES scholarship, where she studied language and culture and taught English.

EMMA HASTINGS is a self-professed Latin nerd, lover of ancient myths, and student of science in addition to being a writer. She draws inspiration for her stories from sources as diverse as scientific articles, conversations overheard on the street, and stories in old newspapers.

EMMA HENSON is 10% Floridian disregard toward punctuality, 40% Pat Conroy novels, 15% breakfast food, 30% HBO shows, 20% couplets of adjectives, and then just dilute with coffee until you're comfortable. She writes because words are there, waiting to be a rebellion.

DARRELL HERBERT is very truthful and decisive with his message in his writing. He lives in Brooklyn and is a part of his high school's Creative Writing Club. Darrell has written more than 400 songs, as well as numerous poems.

ELIZABETH HEYM is excited to study engineering at the Ohio State University next year, since math and science give her writing a sense of symmetry and wonder. William Carlos Williams, who she admires as also being a scientist-poet, provides her with her ideology for poetry: "no ideas but in things."

ASHLEY HUANG is a sophomore at Klein Oak High School in Houston, Texas. She draws her inspiration from personal experiences as well as stories related by her parents and friends.

ASHLEY ISRAEL hails from Greenville, South Carolina, where she studies creative writing at the Fine Arts Center. In the fall, she will be attending Warren Wilson College, where she hopes to study sustainable agriculture and writing.

JAE WOO JANG thinks of writing as a sort of an implosion—as a waterlogged sac ready to burst—and every sentence an adventurous journey of understanding and of transformation. Her own life has been a journey of both realization and transformation: being born in Korea, growing up in Singapore and the Philippines. This fall, she plans to attend Stanford University.

AYLA JEDDY is 13 and lives in New York City. She enjoys writing because it is a unique way to tell and experience powerful stories. Her poems were inspired by an ancient Mesopotamian artifact she encountered in fifth grade at the Penn Museum:

For RYAN JIMENEZ JENKINS, writing allows him to live without walls, and through his pen, his dreams bloom into life. He has a map of the world in his bedroom, where he and his twin sister mark the places they've been and dream about the places they're going to go.

CAROLYN KELLY is a triplet who draws much of her support and inspiration from her family. She is a journalist as well as a creative writer, but likes fiction just a bit more than fact.

WARREN KENNEDY-NOLLE lives in Bedford, New York— about 30 miles from Newtown, Connecticut. He wrote his work in grief and anger over what happened there and this country's subsequent denial, helplessness, and ongoing political buck-passing regarding it. Warren hopes his poem will spark readers to challenge the NRA and this country's broken gun laws.

MAIREAD KILGALLON lives in Bedford Hills, New York. She has always loved reading and imagining situations in which something that didn't occur in a book happened, and that is what motivated her to write. She is now working on a fantasy novel, which is much harder than it seems.

KAIN KIM grew up in Seoul, South Korea, and came to America when she was 6 years old. Her favorite hobby as a child was creating stories on the spot and telling them to anyone who would listen.

MADELEINE LECESNE is enrolled in the Certificate of Artistry Program at Lusher Charter School in New Orleans, Louisiana. She writes because it's the closest she can come to true alchemy.

HALEY LEE was born in Scottsdale, Arizona, 16 years ago. She began writing at a young age and hopes to one day publish a novel. A few of her other goals include opening a food truck, learning how to scuba dive, and teaching English abroad.

MICHAL LEIBOWITZ is from White Plains, New York. Inspired by literary idols Jennifer Egan and Junot Diaz, she writes about everything she knows as well as some things she doesn't. Michal plans to continue writing, this fall at Stanford University.

AILEEN MA writes poetry because sometimes there's a thought in her head that needs to be expressed in some way and yelling it out loud in the middle of the night seems like a surefire way to get the neighbors to dislike her. In all seriousness, writing has helped her express her thoughts, and being able to share something she wrote and see it become more than a mess of thoughts scrambled together is an honor.

EMILY MACK attends Northside College Prep in Chicago. She uses writing to find meaning in life's events. Since first grade, *Citizen Kane* has been her favorite movie.

CARA MAINES is from Houston, Texas, where she is heavily involved in her school newspaper and dance. Her writing is inspired by the told and untold stories of the people around her, and she is motivated by questions of identity and longing.

SARAH MUGHAL is a high-school sophomore living in the middle of nowhere with her books, her computer, and people who tell her to do the dishes. In her spare time she likes to read, ride bikes, and disappear into other dimensions.

GREGORY NAM lives in Durham, Maine. Ever since he was very young (even before he could write!), he loved telling stories. He hopes to be a professional writer someday, and is also interested in biotechnology.

FRANCESCA PARIS is from Oakland, California, and will attend Williams College. She is inspired by Aaron Sorkin, Tracy Kidder, travel, and ripe pomegranates. She would like to thank Andy Spear for his guidance and friendship.

VIVIANA PRADO-NUÑEZ is a sophomore at the George Washington Carver Center for Arts and Technology in Towson, Maryland. Born in San Juan, Puerto Rico, Viviana moved to Maryland at the age of 5 and entered a French immersion program, all of which would later come to influence much of her writing.

JACK RAYSON is 18 years old and was born and raised in Nashville, Tennessee. He writes mostly plays or fiction. He hopes to someday write a children's novel and own a bow. He considers the two to go hand-in-hand.

LATROY ROBINSON is a senior who has spent the majority of high school as part of his school's spoken word club, and this year he made his school's Louder Than a Bomb slam team. He always finds that his writing surprises him in a good way after he reads a good book of poetry.

For rising high-school freshman **CAMILA SANMIGUEL**, writing is her form of retaining sanity: It lets her breathe. From border-city Laredo, Texas, she graduated as salutatorian of her eighth-grade class. She dances, avidly plays piano, listens to alternative music, and always, she writes.

KELLEY SCHLISE lives in Milwaukee, Wisconsin, and enjoys describing specific experiences with great sensory detail in her writing. Her award-winning work, "Memoir of Imagination," was inspired by the carefree feelings she felt when she let her imagination explore new realms.

MICHAEL SHORRIS is a teenager by day and aspiring writer by night, infatuated with his native New York City. He writes to search for that which eludes him and to process that which intimidates him, and he finds sporadic success.

KYNA SMITH attends Cab Calloway School of the Arts in Wilmington, Delaware. As a writer, she is inspired by the fragility of human emotion. Poetry enables her to depict vulnerability and the prevalent fears that many individuals face today.

CLAY SPACE says about himself: Where we live in life helps create how we define ourselves. Me, I'm New Mexican.

ALANA SPENDLEY lives in New Jersey. She does her best imagining when walking the dog or in the shower, and she likes to write about connections and transitions. She will attend Fordham University this fall.

ANNA SUDDERTH is from Fort Worth, Texas. In her poetry, she seeks to find what is strange or out-of-balance in mundane experience and bring that to the surface. In the fall, Anna will be a senior at Trinity Valley School, where her favorite subjects include Chemistry and Creative Writing.

ORIANA TANG is a student at Livingston High School in New Jersey. In addition to winning a Scholastic Art & Writing Award, her writing has been recognized by the National YoungArts Foundation, Foyle Young Poets, among others.

JULIA TOMPKINS loves to write most about her family, all the stories that have woven together to create her life as she knows it. When she isn't writing, she can be found grilling her extended family for material.

JACKSON TRICE is from Greenville, South Carolina. When she's not writing, getting anxious about writing, or telling her mother about her writing, she's drinking Starbucks coffee or forgetting something important. She will attend Amherst College.

CAROLINE TSAI is motivated to write by ideas conceived in the shower and the made-up stories of strangers, as well as the work of John Green, J. K. Rowling, Edna St. Vincent Millay, F. Scott Fitzgerald, T.S. Eliot, and James Kennedy.

RONA WANG lives in Portland, Oregon, where she spends many days listening to rain pitter-patter on the roof while typing away at her laptop. Her writing is inspired by the vibrant people of the city, as well as delicious chai tea lattes.

AUSTIN WEI hails from Clyde Hill, Washington. When he began writing, he was looking for a medium in which he could express his feelings since he was a relatively introverted person. In the future, he hopes to be an entrepreneur, investor, and revolutionary developer in future technologies.

A teacher of JUSTIN WISNICKI'S once told him that you feel no pain when you laugh. When he writes, he keeps this in mind and hopes that, even if only for a minute, he can make his reader feel no pain.

ROBERT ELLIOTT WYATT comes from Denver, Colorado. For Robert, writing is a creative outlet and communication tool. His lifelong love of strange characters and creatures inspired "The Walrus" and other poems. He hopes to become a professional artist and writer.

JACKIE YANG is a graduate of King High School in Tampa, Florida. She enjoys putting off her homework by singing along to Etta James, making crêpes, and reading feminist manifestos.

JADE YOUNG just finished eighth grade at Lakeside Middle School in Seattle, Washington. Her award-winning piece, "Unconfined," involves one of the three criteria the Awards look for: the emergence of her personal voice!

Although he's quite fond of sappy love poems, ALEXANDER ZHANG is most interested in how he can use writing to explore his Asian-American identity, to find a compromise between his Chinese roots and his Southern upbringing.

CHRISTOPHER ZHENG lives in Denver, Colorado, where he spends his time writing, painting, hiking, skiing, or fighting dragons in far-off lands. He would like to thank his teachers for their continuous support and his friends for inspiring him every day.

A TEACHER'S GUIDE TO THE BEST TEEN WRITING OF 2014

These exercises have been adapted from materials developed with the National Writing Project. Use the works of these award-winning teen writers to inspire discussion and guide writing exercises with students.

1. **Short Story: Discussion on characterization and voice— 35 minutes**

   Goal: Students explain how authors establish the voice of a narrator to create distinct characters who inform a reader of time, place, and mood.

   Activity: Introduce the concept of a story's "voice" by having students discuss popular first-person narratives as well as close third-person narratives that are particularly different and compelling.

   Next, choose a piece with highly engaging character voice(s). As you're reading out loud, have students mark any points in the text where they notice specific character establishment through the tone of the prose, dialects, slang, humor, and other details. After you're finished, have students discuss the following:

   • What does the author want us to know or understand about the narrator of this story?

   • How does the separation of character voices establish a reliable—or unreliable—narrator?

   In partners or groups, have students select a narrator and describe his or her personality. Then have them return to the text and find specific details (speech, thought, and interaction with others) to illustrate the narrator's personality and how it informs and shapes the narrative. Share student responses.

2. **Short Story: Writing with focus on characterizing the narrative—35 minutes**

   Goal: Students restructure a narrative with another narrator, creating the same story with a different perspective.

   Activity: Ask students to take on the voice of one of the other characters in the story and tell the story from that point of view, filling in blanks that the original narrator left. Challenge students to use the important characterizing details you found in the reading to give color to their entries.

3. **Poetry: Discussion with focus on form—30 minutes**

   Goal: Students explain how the form (rhyme, line break, syntax) changes the effect and meaning of a poem.

   Activity: Compare a prose poem such as Stephanie Guo's "Insomnia" (p. 160) with a poem that relies heavily on line breaks for emphasis, such as Warren Kennedy-Nolle's "The Two O's of Eyes" (p. 198). How is rhythm created by these two different techniques?

4. **Poetry: Writing with focus on form—30 minutes**

   Goal: Students write using different structural techniques.

   Activity: Have students write two poems on one topic of their choosing. Begin with a prose poem, in which they write freely on that topic; then have them write another poem on the same topic with a focus on line breaks to emphasize changes in rhythm or highlight specific phrases. Discuss the differences after sharing the results.

5. **Personal Essay / Memoir: Writing with a focus on structure and pacing—45 minutes**

Goal: Students will write an organized and coherent memoir imitating the format of a *Best Teen Writing* piece.

Activity: Read "Lessons My Mother Taught Me" by Caroline Tsai (p. 37) out loud with your students. Talk about the format in which her memories are written. Discuss the choices made and how these definitions are inherently personal, therefore inherently suited to convey a personal essay.

Ask your students to write their own memoir modeled after hers.

Consider the decisions each student makes with the following in mind:

• What nouns are so important to the student's memories that they are included in this dictionary-style memoir?

• What does the choice of definitions say about the author of the dictionary-style memoir? How do those choices convey something personal to the reader?

6. **Genre-Shifting Exercise—40 minutes**

Goal: Students will explore form's relationship to function by converting a piece in the anthology to another genre. For example, they will reimagine a play as a poem; a personal essay / memoir as a science fiction / fantasy piece; or a short story as a piece of journalism, reporting on the events therein.

Activity: Have the students choose a favorite piece in *The Best Teen Writing of 2014*, then have them reinterpret that work in another genre. Afterward, have the students compare the original to the genre-shifted piece, and discuss how the same information is relayed through contrasting forms.

7. **Blog Exercise—40 minutes and homework time**

    Goal: Students will use critical thinking skills to offer critiques and analysis of specific works or the anthology.

    Activity: Ask students to write a blog post expressing thoughts about a specific piece of their choosing. Posts will be sent to the Alliance and may be included on the Alliance blog.

    • Students should express their opinions, offering positive feedback or constructive criticism, for a specific work in *The Best Teen Writing*. Alternatively, they may discuss the anthology as a whole.

    • Posts may be emailed to **info@artandwriting.org**, with the subject line "BTW blog post."

REGIONAL AFFILIATE ORGANIZATIONS

The Alliance would like to thank the regional affiliates listed for coordinating the Scholastic Art & Writing Awards.

Northeast

Connecticut
Connecticut Art Region
Affiliate: Connecticut Art Education Association

District of Columbia
DC Metro Writing Region
Affiliate: Writopia Lab

Delaware
Delaware Art Region
Affiliate: Delaware State University

Delaware Writing Region
Affiliate: National League of American Pen Women, Diamond State Branch

Maine
Southern Maine Writing Region
Affiliate: Southern Maine Writing Project

Massachusetts
Massachusetts Art & Writing Region
Affiliate: School of the Museum of Fine Arts (SMFA) and *The Boston Globe*

New Hampshire
New Hampshire Art Region
Affiliate: The New Hampshire Art Educators' Association

New Hampshire Writing Region
Affiliate: Plymouth Writing Project

New Jersey
Northeast New Jersey Art Region
Affiliate: Montclair Art Museum

New York
Central New York Art Region
Affiliate: CNY Art Council, Inc.

Hudson Valley Art Region
Affiliate: Hudson Valley Art Awards

Hudson-to-Housatonic Writing Region
Affiliate: Writopia Lab Westchester & Fairfield

New York City Art & Writing Region
Affiliate: Casita Maria Center for Arts and Education

Twin Tiers Art Region
Affiliate: Arnot Art Museum
(serving parts of New York and Pennsylvania)

Pennsylvania
Berks, Carbon, Lehigh and Northampton Art Region
Affiliate: East Central PA Scholastic Art Awards

Lancaster County Art Region
Affiliate: Lancaster Museum of Art

Lancaster County Writing Region
Affiliate: Lancaster Public Library

Northeastern Pennsylvania Art Region
Affiliate: *The Times-Tribune*

Philadelphia Art Region
Affiliate: Philadelphia Arts in Education Partnership at
the University of the Arts

Philadelphia Writing Region
Affiliate: Philadelphia Writing Project

Pittsburgh Art Region
Affiliate: La Roche College & North Allegheny School District

Pittsburgh Writing Region
Affiliate: Western PA Writing Project

South Central Pennsylvania Art & Writing Region
Affiliate: Commonwealth Connections Academy

Southwestern Pennsylvania Art & Writing Region
Affiliate: California University of Pennsylvania

Rhode Island
Rhode Island Art Region
Affiliate: Rhode Island Art Education Association

Vermont
Vermont Art & Writing Region
Affiliate: Brattleboro Museum & Art Center

Southeast

Florida
Broward Art Region
Affiliate: Young at Art Museum

Central Florida Writing Region
Affiliate: The English Teacher's Friend

Miami-Dade Art Region
Affiliate: Miami-Dade County Public Schools

Miami-Dade Writing Region
Affiliate: Miami Writes

Northeast Florida Art Region
Affiliate: Duval Art Teachers' Association

Palm Beach Art Region
Affiliate: Educational Gallery Group (Eg2)

Pinellas Art Region
Affiliate: Pinellas County Schools

Sarasota Art Region
Affiliate: Sarasota County Schools

Georgia
Georgia Art & Writing Region
Affiliate: Savannah College of Art and Design (SCAD)

Kentucky
Louisville Metropolitan Area Art Region
Affiliate: Jefferson County Public Schools

Northern Kentucky Writing Region
Affiliate: Northern Kentucky Writing Region

South Central Kentucky Art Region
Affiliate: Southern Kentucky Performing Arts Center

Mississippi
Mississippi Art Region
Affiliate: Mississippi Museum of Art

Mississippi Writing Region
Affiliate: The Eudora Welty Foundation

North Carolina
Eastern/Central North Carolina Art Region
Affiliate: Barton College

Mid-Carolina Art & Writing Region
Affiliate: Charlotte-Mecklenburg Schools

Western North Carolina Art Region
Affiliate: Asheville Art Museum

Tennessee
Middle Tennessee Art Region
Affiliate: Cheekwood Botanical Garden & Museum of Art

Mid-South Art Region
Affiliate: Memphis Brooks Museum of Art

Virginia
Arlington County Art Region
Affiliate: Arlington Public Schools

Fairfax County Art Region
Affiliate: Fairfax County Public Schools

Richmond County Art Region
Affiliate: Virginia Museum of Fine Arts

Southwest Virginia Art Region
Affiliate: The Fine Arts Center for the New River Valley

West

California
California Art Region
Affiliate: The California Arts Project

Colorado
Colorado Art Region
Affiliate: Colorado Art Education Association

Hawaii
Hawaii Art Region
Affiliate: Hawaii State Department of Education

Idaho
Idaho Writing Region
Affiliate: Boise State Writing Project

Nevada
Northern Nevada Art Region
Affiliate: The Nevada Museum of Art

Northern Nevada Writing Region
Affiliate: Nevada Alliance for Arts Education

Southern Nevada Art & Writing Region
Affiliate: Springs Preserve

Oregon
Oregon Art Region—Central Oregon Area
Affiliate: The Oregon Art Education Association

Oregon Art Region—Portland Metro Area
Affiliate: The Oregon Art Education Association

Oregon Art Region—Willamette Valley Art Region
Affiliate: Benton County Historical Society

Washington
Snohomish County Art Region
Affiliate: Schack Art Center

Midwest

Illinois
Chicago Writing Region
Affiliate: Chicago Area Writing Project

Mid-Central Illinois Art Region
Affiliate: The Regional Scholastic Art Awards Council of
Mid-Central Illinois

Southern Illinois Art Region
Affiliate: John R. and Eleanor R. Mitchell Foundation/
Cedarhurst
Center for the Arts

Suburban Chicago Art Region
Affiliate: Downers Grove North and South High Schools

Indiana
Central/Southern Indiana Art Region
Affiliate: Clowes Memorial Hall of Butler University

Central/Southern Indiana Writing Region
Affiliate: Clowes Memorial Hall of Butler University and
Hoosier Writing Project at IUPUI

Northeast Indiana and Northwest Ohio Art & Writing Region
Affiliate: Fort Wayne Museum of Art

Northwest Indiana and Lower Southwest Michigan
Art Region
Affiliate: South Bend Museum of Art

Iowa
Iowa Art & Writing Region
Affiliate: The Connie Belin & Jacqueline N. Blank International
Center for Gifted Education and Talent Development,
University of Iowa

Kansas
Eastern Kansas Art Region
Affiliate: The Wichita Center for the Arts

Western Kansas Art Region
Affiliate: The Western Kansas Scholastic Art Awards

Michigan
Michigan Thumb Art Region
Affiliate: College for Creative Studies

Southeastern Michigan Art Region
Affiliate: College for Creative Studies

West Central Michigan Art Region
Affiliate: Kendall College of Art and Design of Ferris State
University

Minnesota
Minnesota Art Region
Affiliate: College of Visual Arts

Missouri
Missouri Writing Region
Affiliate: Prairie Lands Writing Project at Missouri
Western State University

Nebraska
Nebraska Art Region
Affiliate: Omaha Public Schools Art Department

Ohio
Central Ohio Art Region
Affiliate: Columbus College of Art & Design

Cuyahoga County Art & Writing Region
Affiliate: The Cleveland Institute of Art

Lorain County Art Region
Affiliate: Lorain County Regional Scholastic Arts Committee

Miami Valley Art Region
Affiliate: K12 Gallery & TEJAS

Northeast Central Ohio Art Region
Affiliate: Kent State University, Stark Campus

Northeastern Ohio Art Region
Affiliate: Youngstown State University, Art Department

Northeastern Ohio Writing Region
Affiliate: Writing Project at Kent State University

Southern Ohio, Northern Kentucky and Southeastern
Indiana Art Region
Affiliate: Art Machine, Inc.

Wisconsin
Milwaukee Writing Region
Affiliate: Still Waters Collective

Southeast Wisconsin Scholastic Writing Region
Affiliate: Harborside Academy

Wisconsin Art Region
Affiliate: The Milwaukee Art Museum

Southwest

Arizona
Arizona Writing Region
Affiliate: Young Authors of Arizona (YAA)

Louisiana
North-Central Louisiana Writing Region
Affiliate: Northwestern State University Writing Project

Southeast Louisiana Writing Region
Affiliate: Greater New Orleans Writing Project

Oklahoma
Oklahoma Art Region
Affiliate: Tulsa Community College Liberal Arts Department

Oklahoma Writing Region
Affiliate: Tulsa Community College Foundation
and Oklahoma Young Writers

Texas
Harris County Art & Writing Region
Affiliate: Harris County Department of Education

San Antonio Art Region
Affiliate: SAY Sí (San Antonio Youth Yes)

Travis County Art Region
Affiliate: St. Stephen's School

West Texas Art Region
Affiliate: Wayland Baptist University, Department of Art

ACKNOWLEDGEMENTS

The Alliance for Young Artists & Writers gratefully acknowledges the thousands of educators who encourage students to submit their works to the Scholastic Art & Writing Awards each year and the remarkable students who have the courage to put their art and writing before panels of renowned jurors. We would like to especially recognize the National Writing Project for its far-reaching effects in the writing community and its continued commitment to our program.

In addition, our mission is greatly furthered through special partnerships with the National Art Education Association, the Association of Independent Colleges of Art and Design, and the NAACP's ACT-SO program. As a nonprofit organization, our ability to recognize and honor creative teens across the country is made possible through the generosity of our supporters: Scholastic Inc., the Maurice R. Robinson Fund, Command Web Offset Co., the Institute for Museum and Library Services, the President's Committee on the Arts and the Humanities, The New York Times, Kramer Levin Naftalis & Frankel LLP, the National Endowment for the Arts, Blick Art Materials & Utrecht Art Supplies, 3D Systems, the Gedenk Movement, Golden Artist Colors, Bloomberg L.P., the Bernstein Family Foundation, the New York City Department of Cultural Affairs, Duck Tape®, the Jacques and Natasha Gelman Foundation, Colossal Media, and contributions from numerous individual, foundation, and corporate funders.

SUPPORT THE SCHOLASTIC ART & WRITING AWARDS

The Best Teen Writing is made possible through the generous support of our donors.

Nearly 255,000 works were submitted and judged for the 2014 Awards, and upwards of 68,000 middle and high school artists and writers were recognized for their talents. Of the top national winners in the Awards' eleven writing categories, 71 works are highlighted in this publication.

The Alliance for Young Artists & Writers, which presents the Awards, is a nonprofit 501(c)(3) organization and is supported entirely by charitable contributions from institutional partners and individuals like you. Donations underwrite the production of the Awards at the national and local levels; exhibitions, readings, and workshops; publications; and award and scholarship opportunities for creative young artists and writers in grades 7–12 across the country.

Help us continue to celebrate our nation's most creative teens in both writing and art. Please make your tax-deductible contribution today.

To give online: Visit **www.artandwriting.org/donate**.

To give by check: Mail check, made payable to Alliance for Young Artists & Writers, to:

Alliance for Young Artists & Writers
Attention: Development/External Relations
557 Broadway
New York, NY 10012

To make a special gift or to discuss other ways to provide your financial support, please contact the Alliance for Young Artists & Writers, by phone at 212-343-7700 or by e-mail at **support@artandwriting.org**.